THOUGHT'S EGO

in Augustine and Descartes

Also by Gareth B. Matthews:

Philosophy and the Young Child

Dialogues with Children

Ammonius on Aristotle's "Categories" (trans., with S. Marc Cohen)

GARETH B. MATTHEWS

THOUGHT'S EGO IN AUGUSTINE AND DESCARTES

CORNELL UNIVERSITY PRESS

Ithaca and London

First published 1992 by Cornell University Press.

International Standard Book Number 0-8014-2775-4
Library of Congress Catalog Card Number 92-52767
Printed in the United States of America
*Librarians: Library of Congress cataloging information appears on the last page of
the book.*

⊗ The paper in this book meets the minimum requirements
of the American National Standard for Information Sciences—
Permanence of Paper for Printed Library Material. ANSI Z39.48-1984.

Hector-Neri Castañeda
(1924–1991)
in memoriam

Contents

Preface

"None," Søren Kierkegaard once complained, "none dares say 'I'." Whatever may have been true of Kierkegaard's contemporaries, against whom he directed this remark, certainly both Augustine and Descartes were thinkers who dared say "I." In ways that are strikingly similar, as well as strikingly different, they developed and presented many of their philosophical thoughts from an unapologetically first-person point of view. In this they were worthy of Kierkegaard's approbation.

Aurelius Augustinus (354–430 A.D.) wrote the first significant autobiography in Western culture, his *Confessions*. He also wrote a monologue, the *Soliloquies*, which he cast as a dialogue between himself and reason. Both works are clearly written from a first-person perspective.

After St. Paul, Augustine is arguably the most influential Christian theologian of all time. But he is not widely recognized as a great philosopher. So, although it is certainly clear that he dared say "I," it may seem strange that I propose to examine the role of thought's 'I' in his *philosophy*. Though what I have to say about Augustine should convince my readers that he is a much more interesting and important philosophical thinker than is generally appreciated, I make no claim that he is a philosopher of the first rank. Nor is it surprising that he should be only, so to speak, a major "minor" philosopher, even if someone still worthy of philosophical study. For one thing, Augustine had no formal training in philosophy. He was trained rather as a rhetorician, and he taught rhetoric until his conversion to Christianity at the age of thirty-three. Much of the philosophy that he learned he absorbed from the writings of Cicero, who was not himself a philosophically original thinker. Although in young adulthood Augustine did form a philosophical circle of friends, at which time he also wrote philosophical dialogues, he abandoned such activity when he became a Christian priest, some four years after his conversion. The remainder of his life he devoted to his ministry, first as a parish priest and then as a bishop.

If not then by training or profession, it was rather by character and temperament that Augustine was a philosopher. Without the benefit of an academic environment or the stimulus of astute philosophical colleagues, or students, he managed somehow to pursue his philosophical interests while writing letters, preaching sermons, defining dogma, writing biblical commentaries, and making pronouncements on world history.

Though René Descartes (1596–1650) did not have what we might think of today as advanced training in philosophy, he was certainly well schooled in scholasticism at the Jesuit college of La Flèche; moreover, he carried on philosophical correspondence with some of the most astutely philosophical minds of his day. He was certainly, first and last, a philosopher, indeed, a philosopher of the first rank. In literary form Descartes's two most famous works, the *Discourse on the Method* and the *Meditations on First Philosophy*, are both first-person treatises. The *Discourse* presents itself as an intellectual autobiography, and the *Meditations* is a set of six consecutive first person reflections.

Several of Descartes's contemporaries were struck by the

similarity between the Cartesian cogito and the role of 'I am' in the thought of Augustine. In fact, ever since Descartes's time, scholars have debated the extent and nature of Augustine's influence on Descartes. Though some of what I have to say in the pages to follow bears on that old, and yet seemingly forever new, question of influence, it is not my project here to assess influence.[1] Instead, I want to consider what Augustine and Descartes have to show us about *doing* philosophy from an insistently first-person point of view. For the purposes of my project we need to view each thinker as a teacher in his own right, rather than merely as a follower of someone else or as a product of this influence or that. The question of influence is therefore marginal here.

My aim, then, is to explore "logical space" by exploring a bit of "historical space." By examining the first-personalization of philosophy in these two historical figures, we can learn something important about our own philosophical options, and about those of any other thinker who dares, philosophically, say "I."

ॐ

I began this book in 1986 while a member of the Institute for Advanced Study in Princeton. There I was stimulated and encouraged by wonderful colleagues, including Dagfinn

---

1. Twentieth-century discussion of this issue effectively begins with Etienne Gilson's *Index scolastico-cartésien* (Paris, 1912; rpt. New York: Burt Franklin, Bibliography and Reference series no. 57), and continues with his *Études sur le rôle de la pensée médiévale dans la formation du système cartésien* (Paris: Vrin, 1930; 3d ed., 1967). For a more recent assessment, see Henri Gouhier, *Cartésianisme et augustinisme au XVIIe siècle* (Paris: Vrin, 1978). On the question of influence my own view is very close to that of Léon Blanchet: "It does not appear to us possible that before the publication of the *Meditations* Descartes had not had knowledge, directly or indirectly, at least of the thoughts expressed in the *De trinitate* and very probably of the text, either by reading the work itself, or large quotations furnished by other authors" (*Les antécédents historiques du "Je pense, donc, je suis"* [Paris: Félix Alcan, 1920], 54–55).

Føllesdal, Daniel Garber, and David Norton, but especially by
Morton White, then chair of the School of Historical Studies.
Morton had been one of my favorite professors while I was a
graduate student at Harvard University three decades earlier.
My dean, Murray Schwartz, encouraged by my department
chair, Robert Sleigh, provided financial support for the Institute term.

Three years later, 1989–90, I resumed work on this project
on a fellowship from the National Endowment for the Hu-
manities. Again Dean Schwartz came through with needed
support, encouraged this time by my new department chair,
John Robison. For part of that NEH year Richard Sorabji
afforded me the hospitality of the Centre for Philosophical
Studies, King's College, London. I tried out some of my ideas
on Richard and on his London colleagues. Earlier in the year,
John Fisher had invited me to give three lectures at the University of Colorado on Augustine and Descartes. And on my
return from London, Sheldon Cohen invited me to partici-
pate in a conference on the history of the idea of consciousness at the University of Tennessee, Knoxville.

Among the many people who have commented on parts of
this book in some form or other, Fred Feldman deserves special mention for his early and incisive criticism. Others who
have helped me include Harry Bracken, John Fisher, George
Bealer, Dale Jamieson, Robert Hanna, Lynne Baker, Sheldon
Cohen, Calvin Normore, Richard Sorabji, Myles Burnyeat,
Richard La Croix, and William Mann. Especially helpful in
the last two rounds of revisions was a sympathetic, tough-
minded, and anonymous referee for Cornell University Press.

Part of Chapter 2 appeared in the *Pacific Philosophical Quar-
terly* 68 (1987), 197–204, as "Descartes's *Cogito* and Katz's
Cogitations." A version of Chapter 8 was published as "On
Being Immoral in a Dream," *Philosophy* 56 (1981), 47–54.
And a version of Chapter 9 appeared as "Descartes and the
Problem of Other Minds," in *Essays on Descartes' Meditations,*
ed. Amelia Rorty. (Berkeley: University of California Press,

1986), 141–51. I thank the respective editors and publishers for permission to use that material in this work.

With great respect and affection I dedicate this work to the memory of Hector-Neri Castañeda (1924–91), who died in the very month that it was accepted for publication. In addition to paying tribute to a perversely original thinker and a delightfully memorable personality, I acknowledge gratefully that, without Hector's insistent efforts to get us all to pay attention to the philosophical importance of pronouns in their reflexive use, it would never have occurred to me to develop my topic in the way I have.

GARETH B. MATTHEWS

Amherst, Massachusetts

Translations, Sources, and Abbreviations

Unless otherwise indicated, Augustine's writings are quoted from these translations:

Against the Academics [*Contra academicos*], trans. John J. O'Meara. *Ancient Christian Writers*, no. 12. New York: Newman Press, 1951.

The Catholic Way of Life [*De moribus ecclesiae*], trans. Donald A. Gallagher and Idella J. Gallagher. *Fathers of the Church*, vol. 56. Washington, D.C.: Catholic University of America Press, 1966.

Christian Instruction [*De doctrina christiana*], trans. John J. Gavigan. *Fathers of the Church*, vol. 2. Washington, D.C.: Catholic University of America Press, 1950.

City of God, trans. Gerald G. Walsh et al. Garden City: Image Books, 1958.

Concerning the Teacher [*De magistro*], trans. G. C. Leckie. *Basic Writings of Saint Augustine*, ed. Whitney J. Oates, 1:361–95. New York: Random House, 1948.

Confessions, trans. R. S. Pine-Coffin. Harmondsworth: Penguin, 1961.

Eighty-Three Different Questions [*De diversis quaestionibus LXXXIII*], trans. David L. Mosher. *Fathers of the Church*, vol. 70. Washington, D.C.: Catholic University of America Press, 1982.

Homilies on the Gospel of John [*In joannis evangelium*], trans. John Gibb and James Innes. *A Select Library of the Nicene and Post-Nicene Fathers*, ed. Philip Schaff, 7:7–452. New York: Christian Literature, 1888.

The Immortality of the Soul [*De immortalitate animae*], trans. Ludwig Schopp. New York: Fathers of the Church, 1947, 15–47.

Letters [*Epistola*], trans. Wilfrid Parsons. *Fathers of the Church,* vols. 12, 18, 20, 30, 32. Washington, D.C.: Catholic University of America Press, 1951–56.

The Literal Meaning of Genesis [*De genesi ad litteram*], trans. John Hammond Taylor. *Ancient Christian Writers,* vols. 41–42. New York: Newman Press, 1982.

The Lord's Sermon on the Mount [*De sermone domini in monte*], trans. John J. Jepson. *Ancient Christian Writers,* no. 5. New York: Newman Press, 1948.

Lying [*De mendacio*], in *Treatises on Various Subjects,* trans. Mary Sarah Muldowney. *Fathers of the Church,* 16:47–110. Washington, D.C.: Catholic University of America Press, 1952.

Of True Religion [*De vera religione*], trans. John H. S. Burleigh. *Augustine: Earlier Writings,* in *The Library of Christian Classics,* 6:225–83. Philadelphia: Westminster Press, 1953.

On Free Choice of the Will [*De libero arbitrio*], trans. Anna S. Benjamin and L. H. Hackstaff. Indianapolis: Bobbs-Merrill, 1964.

On Man's Perfection in Righteousness [*De perfectione justiciae hominis*], trans. Peter Holmes et al. *A Select Library of the Nicene and Post-Nicene Fathers,* ed. Philip Schaff, 5:159–76. New York: Christian Literature, 1887.

On the Greatness of the Soul [*De quantitate animae*], trans. Joseph M. Colleran. *Ancient Christian Writers,* no. 9. New York: Newman Press, 1950.

On the Soul and Its Origin [*De anima et ejus origine*], trans. Peter Holmes et al. *A Select Library of the Nicene and Post-Nicene Fathers,* ed. Philip Schaff, 5:315–71. New York: Christian Literature, 1887.

On the Spirit and the Letter [*De spiritu et littera*], trans. P. Holmes. *Basic Writings of Saint Augustine,* ed. Whitney J. Oates, 1:461–518. New York: Random House, 1948.

The Retractions [*Retractiones*], trans. Mary Inez Bogan. *Fathers of the Church,* vol. 60. Washington, D.C.: Catholic University of America Press, 1968.

The Trinity [*De trinitate*], trans. Stephen McKenna. *Fathers of the Church,* vol. 45. Washington, D.C.: Catholic University of America Press, 1963.

The Usefulness of Belief [*De utilitate credendi*], in *Augustine: Earlier Writings,* trans. John H. S. Burleigh. *Library of Christian Classics,* 6:287–323. Philadelphia: Westminster Press, 1953.

All citations of Descartes's works include a reference to the standard edition of Descartes, *Oeuvres de Descartes,* ed. Charles Adam and Paul Tannery, 12 vols. (Paris: Vrin, 1964–76). Following custom, I give those references as "AT" plus the volume and page of the passage.

Most quotations from Descartes are given in the translation of John Cottingham, Robert Stoothoff, and Dugald Murdoch, *The Philosophical Writings of Descartes*, 2 vols. (Cambridge University Press, 1985). I refer to passages in this translation as "CSM" plus the volume and page.

CSM does not include letters. Where possible I take quotations of letters from *Descartes: Philosophical Letters*, trans. Anthony Kenny (Oxford: Clarendon Press, 1970). I cite passages from Kenny's collection as "K" plus the page.

THOUGHT'S EGO
in Augustine and Descartes

[1]

'I*' Questions

Thomas Nagel has characterized the attempt to transcend one's particular view and "to conceive the world as a whole" as an effort to get "the view from nowhere."[1] By contrast, the attempt to do philosophy from an unabashedly first-person point of view might be said to be getting "the view from here," and perhaps helping others get the view from their own "here."

No doubt much of the history of modern philosophy could be presented as a contest for primacy between those who want to describe "the view from nowhere" and those who insist on describing it from their own "here." Interesting as it might be to lay out that contest, it is not my task to do that in this book. Rather, I discuss the role of the ego in the philosophical thought of Augustine and Descartes as it bears on the idea of doing philosophy from one's own "here."

ã

It would be hard to imagine a serious treatise in physics or mathematics that takes the form of presenting the author's

1. Thomas Nagel, *The View from Nowhere* (New York: Oxford University Press, 1986), 3.

autobiography. An autobiographical point of view is at odds with the very activity of doing physics or mathematics. Of course, the rest of us may become fascinated by the personal life of an eminent scientist or mathematician—by the life of Einstein, say, or Newton—but it was part of the professional aim of Einstein and Newton to transcend the perspectives of their personal lives and to achieve in their research and writing an entirely impersonal objectivity.

In doing philosophy, many philosophers likewise eschew a first-person perspective. The questions these philosophers pursue ('What is knowledge?' 'What is time?' 'What is virtue?') are perfectly general and quite impersonal. It is plausible to think that any worthwhile answer to their questions will also be general and impersonal. Third-person questions are, however, often cast in the first person. If I ask,

(1)   Why should one be moral?

my question may not engage my reader's attention as much as would the first-person counterpart,

(2)   Why should I be moral?

But what is at stake here, I should say, is little more than rhetorical effectiveness. If I ask (2) in a philosophically serious way, my question is practically equivalent to the third-person question, (1). What I mean by 'practical equivalence' is that any good candidate for an answer to one of those two questions can easily be turned into an equally good candidate for an answer to the other; no special thought or expertise beyond a linguistic ability to make the needed grammatical changes is required for the transformation. If (1) and (2) are indeed practically equivalent, as I take them to be, it is presumably because any satisfactory answer to (2) is a general answer that applies equally to everyone. The presumption that this is so is rooted in the idea that being ethical requires one to assume an impersonal perspective, a perspective from which each person is to be treated as, in a certain way, interchangeable with every other person.

Some questions in philosophy, however, are clearly much more solidly first-personal than (2). Among the most interesting of these are questions that are naturally expressed through a reflexive use of the singular first-person pronouns, 'I', 'me', 'my', and 'myself'. Here are some examples:[2]

(3)   Can I be certain that I (myself) exist?
(4)   How do I know that I (myself) am not now dreaming?
(5)   Can I know that there are minds in addition to my own (i.e., in addition to the one I, myself, have)?

Several philosophers, including Peter Geach, Hector Castañeda, John Perry, David Lewis, and Roderick Chisholm, have called our attention to the importance of the reflexive use of personal pronouns, especially in contexts in which they are governed by 'know', 'believe', and closely related verbs.[3] Elizabeth Anscombe has emphasized the reflexive use of *first*-person pronouns in particular and has linked that use to central reasoning in Augustine and Descartes.[4]

2. Although 'I' is not classified as a reflexive pronoun the way 'myself' is, 'I' may still be *used* reflexively—as indeed it is in its second occurrence in each of these questions. It is the reflexive *use* of personal pronouns I am interested in here.

3. P. T. Geach, "Intentionality: On Beliefs about Oneself," in *Logic Matters* (Oxford: Blackwell, 1972), 128–29. Hector-Neri Castañeda, "He: A Study in the Logic of Self-Consciousness," *Ratio* 8 (1966), 130–57; "Indicators and Quasi-indicators," *American Philosophical Quarterly* 4 (1967), 85–100; "On the Logic of Attributions of Self-Knowledge to Others," *Journal of Philosophy* 65 (1968), 439–56. John Perry, "The Essential Indexical," *Nous* 13 (1979), 3–21. David Lewis, "Attitudes De Dicto and De Se," *Philosophical Review* 88 (1979), 513–43. Roderick Chisholm, *The First Person: An Essay on Reference and Intentionality* (Minneapolis: University of Minnesota Press, 1981), especially chapter 3.

4. G. E. M. Anscombe, "The First Person," in *Mind and Language*, ed. Samuel Guttenplan (Oxford: Clarendon Press, 1975), 45–65.

Castañeda marks off the reflexive use of 'he' by writing that
pronoun, when it is so used, as "he*." Following him, I refer
to singular first-person pronouns in their reflexive use as "'I*'
pronouns" (pronounced "I-star pronouns").
The position an 'I*' pronoun occupies in a sentence or
statement is referentially opaque. Thus, from 'I know that I
exist' and 'I am Gary Matthews', or 'I am the author of this
book', these do not follow: 'I know that Gary Matthews exists'.
'I know that the author of this book exists'. I may know that I
exist but, suffering from amnesia, not know that I am Gary
Matthews, or that I wrote this book. 'I*' pronouns, indeed
personal pronouns generally, when they are used reflexively,
seem to pick out subjects from the individual subject's own
point of view, and not under any particular name or definite
description either.[5] They seem to pick out what I call
"thought's ego."
Because the reflexive use of third-person pronouns preserves the subject's point of view, turning an 'I*' question into
a 'she*', 'he*', or 'one*' question therefore does not obliterate
the subject's point of view; instead, it preserves it. Consider an
example. Suppose one were to say that any satisfactory justification for answering 'yes' to

(3')   Can I be certain that I* exist?

would automatically provide the materials for answering 'yes'
to the third-personal question,

(6)   Can one be certain that one* exists?

Would that mean that (3') is not seriously first-personal? Not
at all. The generality of (6) does not obliterate the first-person
point of view; rather, it preserves that point of view. Question
(6) does not mean

5. For a discussion of this point, see the works cited in note 3.

(7)   Can anyone, for example, Jones, be certain that he (Jones) exists?

Jones, for example, may be certain that he* exists without being certain that Jones exists (not realizing that he is Jones). What Jones is certain of is "I exist." As Peter Geach writes, "'he himself' [is] an *oratio obliqua* [indirect speech] proxy for the first-person pronoun of *oratio recta* [direct speech]."[6] Accordingly, (6) is an indirect-speech version of something like this:

(8)   Can one be certain of this: "I exist"?

In an important way, then, 'I*' questions are irreducibly first-personal. Even if we suppose that any good answer (to pick another important 'I*' question) to

(4')   How do I know that I* am not now dreaming?

automatically provides the materials for a good answer to the third-person question

(9)   How does one know that one* is not now dreaming?

it does not follow that the first-personalism of (4') is, in any serious way, eliminable by appeal to (9). For (9), unlike (1), preserves the first-person point of view of the subjects it applies to through the use of the reflexively used pronoun 'one*'. It is an indirect-discourse version of

(10)   How does one know this: "I am not now dreaming"?

One thing that makes all this relevant to the study at hand is something we might call the "paradox of first-person philoso-

6. Geach, "Intentionality," 129.

phy." If it is important for me to do philosophy from a first-person point of view (as it seems to have been important for both Augustine and Descartes), it is important for me to write in the first person, indeed, in the first person singular. Yet, if it is worthwhile for me to write my thoughts down at all, it is presumably important because my thoughts have application to others. That application to others can, one would suppose, be put in general, third-person statements. But then if the application of what I have to say can be put in third-person statements, I need not, except perhaps for rhetorical purposes, have written in the first person after all.

One way to escape the horns of this dilemma is to focus on 'I*' questions. Their generalizations—'she*', 'he*', and 'one*' questions—and the answers to them preserve the first-person point of view. So, I can contentedly go on writing in the first person and allow my questions and answers to be generalized without having to worry that their first-person point of view will be destroyed.

જ

I do not mean to suggest that all 'I*' questions are philosophically interesting; that is certainly not the case. 'How do I know where I* am going to get my next meal?' may be of great prudential interest to me personally. In fact, preoccupation with this 'I*' question may even prevent me from turning my attention to philosophy. But, in and of itself, the question has no special philosophical importance.

Some 'I*' questions, however, clearly have great philosophical importance. And prominent among them are questions to which the writings of Augustine and Descartes direct our attention. In fact, among the 'I*' questions to which Augustine and Descartes direct our attention are some of the most philosophically fascinating questions there are:

(i)   Can I doubt whether I* exist? (Chapters 2, 3)
(ii) What can I know, or be certain, that I* am? (Chapter 4)

(iii)   How do I know whether I* am now dreaming?
        (Chapters 5, 7)
(iv)   How do I know that not all life is my dream, that is,
        that not all life is a dream I* am having? (Chapters 6,
        7)
(v)   Am I morally responsible for what I* think and do in
        my dreams? (Chapter 8)
(vi)   How do I know, or how do I come to believe, that
        there are minds in addition to my own, that is, in
        addition to the one I* have? (Chapter 9)

These six questions concern thought's ego. In saying this, I
use the expression 'thought's ego' for *whatever is referred to, or
seems to be referred to,* by the 'I*' in these 'I*' questions.

Some philosophers, Elizabeth Anscombe for one, have denied that 'I' is a referring expression at all. Indeed, it is the
peculiarity of 'I' in its 'I*' uses that leads Anscombe to insist
that "'I' is neither a name nor another kind of expression
whose logical role is to make a reference, *at all*."[7] I take no
stand on this issue. Clearly, however, 'I' *seems*, at least, to be a
referring expression. In its reflexive uses, that is, as 'I*', it
seems to pick out a thinking subject from that subject's own
point of view, and in such a way that the subject can have
direct and unimpeachable knowledge of its identity, perhaps
even of its nature. Augustine's and Descartes's attention to this
seemingly privileged reference and to the subject it seems to
pick out is my topic for this book.

If, pace Anscombe, 'I' is a genuine referring expression,
does it pick out a different object in its reflexive use, that is, as
'I*', from the one it picks out in its nonreflexive uses? A consideration that might tempt one to say "yes" to this question is
the observation that from

(11)   I can be certain that I* exist

plus the simple identity claim

7. Anscombe, "First Person," 60.

(12) I am Gary Matthews

I may conclude

(13) Gary Matthews can be certain that he* exists.

Yet, to go validly from (11) to

(14) I can be certain that Gary Matthews exists

I need something more than the identity claim (12)—
something such as this:

(15) I am certain that I am Gary Matthews.

Since to license the substitution of 'Gary Matthews' for 'I' in
(11) I need only a simple identity claim, whereas something
more is required to license the substitution of 'Gary Matthews'
for 'I*', 'I' and 'I*' in (11) do not have exactly the same refer-
ent. So, at any rate, the reasoning might go.

On the other side, it seems clear that (11) ought to be an
assurance to me of my own existence, and not merely an
assurance to me that some inner shadow self of mine exists.
So (11) ought to be open to a reading according to which 'I'
and 'I*' pick out the very same subject (as we see later, Descartes supposes this to be the case).

Again, I take no stand on this issue. The point is that many
'I*' questions, especially the ones listed above, seem to focus
attention on a subject from that subject's own point of view.[8]

---

8. Granted that my earlier "next-meal" question is philosophically unin-
teresting, does the 'I*' in it even *seem* to pick out a subject from that subject's
own point of view? On first thought, one wants to say "no." But there is a
second thought. Suppose I am considering the skeptical question, 'How do I
know that I* am not a brain in a vat, or a disembodied spirit?' Suppose
further that, feeling a pang of hunger, I interrupt my philosophical reflec-

How they do this, and what it is to be a subject from its own point of view, are matters for philosophical investigation. Highly relevant to such an investigation are the writings of Augustine and Descartes.

My talk in this book about thought's ego can always be translated into talk about 'I*' questions; I use the terminology of 'thought's ego' simply as a way of calling attention to the phenomenon of philosophically interesting 'I*' questions. And so my topic for the book, thought's ego in the philosophies of Augustine and Descartes, is equally this: interesting 'I*' Questions in the philosophies of Augustine and Descartes.

I do not mean to suggest that Augustine and Descartes exhausted the 'I*' questions that might interest a philosopher; that is surely not true. When John Locke tried to tell us what 'person' stands for ("a thinking intelligent being, that has reason and reflection, and can consider itself as itself, the same thinking thing, in different times and places")[9], he invited us to ask philosophically interesting questions like this one: 'How do I know whether I* am the same person as the boy who was flogged at school for robbing an orchard?'[10] In inviting us to reflect on 'I*' questions like that, Locke introduced the discussion of personal identity through time as a philosophical

tions to ask, "How do I know where I* am going to get my next meal?" In a mood of what one might call "metaphysical gallows humor," I might reason as follows: "If I am a brain in a vat, let alone a disembodied spirit, it can be of no use to me to worry about how I* am going to get my next meal." In such a context, the idea that 'I*' in the "next-meal" question might refer to thought's ego becomes somewhat more plausible.

My suspicion is that, for any 'I*' question—even the most mundane—a philosophical context could be invented in which the 'I*' in that question seems to pick out a subject from that subject's own point of view. Still, in their philosophically unenriched contexts, such 'I*' questions could hardly be said to have that function.

9. John Locke, *Essay Concerning Human Understanding*, chap. 27, sec. 9.
10. I am adapting Thomas Reid's famous counterexample to Locke in Reid's *Essays on the Intellectual Powers of Man* (Edinburgh, 1785), chap. 6 ("Of Memory").

problem. That problem, which has provoked a great deal of interesting discussion by philosophers in recent years, is not to be found in either Augustine or Descartes.

Although Augustine and Descartes did not exhaust the 'I*' questions that might be of philosophical interest, they did manage, between them, to raise several 'I*' questions of cardinal philosophical importance. It is my project here to understand the role these questions play in their respective philosophies. Since, as it turns out, the role of thought's ego in Augustine's philosophy is different from its role in Descartes's, comparison of the two also helps us understand each one singly.

I begin with the most famous 'I*' question of all, 'Can I doubt that I* exist?' Since it is Descartes who made that question famous, I begin with his treatment of it and the answer he gave it. But, although the main focus of the next chapter is Descartes, it is also important to keep Augustine in the picture right from the beginning.

[2]

The Cartesian Cogito

'Cogito, ergo sum' is perhaps the most famous sentence in all philosophy. It seems peculiarly modern. Certainly the concepts, the lines of reasoning, and the intellectual orientation that go with it form a framework for characteristically modern ideas about minds, bodies, and knowledge. Despite the stamp of modernity on the cogito, and the stamp of the cogito on modernity, Descartes's famous idea was not entirely original with him. Among Descartes's own contemporaries, Mersenne, Colvius, and Arnauld all pointed out that the cogito resembles reasoning to be found in the writings of Augustine over twelve centuries earlier.[1] Arnauld mentions specifically as a parallel to Descartes this passage from Augustine's *On Free Choice of the Will:* "Therefore, to start at the beginning with the most obvious, I will ask you whether you yourself exist. Are you, perhaps, afraid that you are being deceived by my questioning? But if you did not exist, it would be impossible for you to be deceived" (II.3). The similarity to Descartes is evident: "But there is a deceiver

1. For Mersenne, see Descartes's letter to Mersenne, 25 May [?]; AT 1: 376. For Colvius, see Descartes's letter to Colvius, 14 November, 1640; AT 3: 247; K, 83–84. For Arnauld, see Objections IV; AT 7: 198; CSM 2: 139. For an extensive discussion of these matters, see Henri Gouhier, *Cartésianisme et Augustinisme au XVIIe siècle* (Paris: Vrin, 1978).

of supreme power and cunning who is deliberately and constantly deceiving me. In that case I too undoubtedly exist, if he is deceiving me" (Meditation II; AT VII, 25; CSM II, 17). Even more striking are the parallels between the Cartesian cogito and a passage from the *City of God* (XI.26) we examine in the next chapter, which Mersenne had mentioned. Reflecting on these parallels, one might wonder whether Augustine's ideas simply had a delayed effect. Could it be that they have modern Cartesianism as their full implication but no one drew that implication until Descartes wrote the *Discourse* and *Meditations* over 1200 years after Augustine's death? I do not try to answer that question until later in this book. My immediate aim is to cast some light on the cogito in Descartes and then, especially in the next chapter, on the relationship between the cogito in Descartes and cogito-like passages in Augustine.

Since the similarity between his cogito and certain reasoning in Augustine was pointed out to Descartes by several of his contemporaries, and since Descartes tried to say for himself something about this similarity, we might begin by looking at Descartes's own responses to get a little clearer about the relationship. This following passage from a letter to Colvius gives us what is perhaps Descartes's most interesting attempt to set the matter straight:

> I am obliged to you for drawing my attention to the passage of St. Augustine relevant to my [*I think, therefore I am*]. I went today to the library of this town to read it, and I find that he does really use it to prove the certainty of our existence. He goes on to show that there is a certain likeness of the Trinity in us, in that we exist, we know that we exist, and we love the existence and the knowledge we have. I, on the other hand, use the argument to show that this I which is thinking is an immaterial substance with no bodily element. These are two very different things. In

itself it is such a simple and natural thing to infer that one exists from the fact that one is doubting that it could have occurred to any writer. But I am very glad to find myself in agreement with St. Augustine, if only to hush the little minds who have tried to find fault with the principle. (Descartes to Colvius, 14 November 1640; AT III, 247; K, 83–84)

This passage is remarkable for at least these three reasons: First, it suggests that before 1640, three years after he had published his *Discourse,* in which 'cogito, ergo sum' appears for the first time, Descartes had never read either Book XV of Augustine's *Trinity,* which is the principal work in which Augustine finds a likeness between his mind and the divine Trinity, or Book XI of the *City of God,* where the Trinity analogy is also coupled with cogito-like reasoning. Both the nature of Descartes's Jesuit education at La Flèche and the strong similarities between passages in Descartes and passages in both the *Trinity* and the *City of God* make such innocence seem quite unlikely.

The passage also suggests in a surprisingly flat-footed way that the point of the cogito is "to infer that one exists from the fact that one is doubting" and "to prove with certainty that one exists." Considering the vast amount of ingenuity lavished by recent commentators on the cogito and the great subtlety achieved in some of their interpretations, Descartes's own account of his famous idea seems unwelcomely crude, almost dismissive.

Third, the passage suggests that the most significant difference between 'cogito, ergo sum' in Descartes and similar reasoning in Augustine is that the former, but not the latter, is used to establish that "this I which is thinking is an immaterial substance with no bodily element."

Let us consider the last point first. I assume that Descartes was adverting to such bits of his own reasoning as this:

I saw that while I could pretend that I had no body and that there was no world and no place for me to be in, I could not for all that pretend that I did not exist. I saw on the contrary that from the mere fact that I thought of doubting the truth of other things, it followed quite evidently and certainly that I existed; whereas if I had merely ceased thinking, even if everything else I had ever imagined had been true, I should have had no reason to believe that I existed. From this I knew I was a substance whose whole essence or nature is simply to think, and which does not require any place, or depend on any material thing, in order to exist. Accordingly this 'I'—that is, the soul by which I am what I am—is entirely distinct from the body, and indeed is easier to know than the body. (*Discourse*, Part IV; AT VI, 32–33; CSM I, 127)

Or this:

> I am not that structure of limbs which is called a human body. I am not even some thin vapour which permeates the limbs—a wind, fire, air, breath, or whatever I depict in my imagination; for these are things which I have supposed to be nothing. Let this supposition stand; for all that I am still something. (Meditation II; AT VII, 27; CSM II, 18)

The curious thing is that there is similar reasoning in Augustine's *Trinity*. To be sure, it is not in Book XV, the primary locus in that work for cogito-like reasoning; instead it is in Book X. But there is also cogito-like reasoning even in Book X, as in these passages:

> And no one doubts that no one understands who does not live, and that no one lives who does not exist. (*Trinity*, X.10.13)

> On the other hand who would doubt that he lives, remembers, understands, wills, thinks, knows, and judges? For even if he doubts, he lives. *Trinity*, X.10.14)

Compare Descartes:

> But what then am I? A thing that thinks. What is that? A thing that doubts, understands, affirms, denies, is willing, is unwill-

ing, and also imagines and has sensory perceptions. (AT VII, 28; CSM II, 19)

The passages above from Augustine are followed, two paragraphs later, by this:

[N]othing is at all rightly said to be known while its substance is not known. And therefore, when the mind knows itself, it knows its own substance; and when it is certain about itself, it is certain about its own substance. But it is certain about itself, as those things which are said above prove convincingly; although it is not at all certain whether itself is air, or fire, or some body, or some function of body. Therefore it is not any of these. And to that whole which is bidden to know itself, belongs this, that it is certain that it is not any of those things of which it is uncertain, and is certain that it is that only, which only it is certain that it is. (*Trinity,* X.10.16)

We are left with the surprising conclusion that, by Descartes's own account, cogito-like reasoning in Augustine is like cogito reasoning in Descartes in being a proof of one's own existence—and, contrary to Descartes's claim, it is also like Descartes's reasoning in being used to "show that this I which is thinking is an immaterial substance with no bodily element." Thus the cogito in Descartes is no different from the cogito in his fourth-century predecessor. Can this be right?

I think not. Indisputably, Descartes was a great philosopher. Whether he was also a great historian of philosophy is something else. The evidence of the letter to Colvius suggests not.

❧

To sort things out a bit, let us now review the main current ways of interpreting Descartes's cogito. Any serious student of Descartes today faces a daunting array of highly sophisticated interpretations of the cogito. These interpretations differ`in interesting and often complex ways. One reason for the disagreement among commentators is the striking difference between the two key passages in which Descartes presents his cogito, namely, the one in Part IV of the *Discourse* and the one in Meditation II. Here they are:

> I noticed that while I was trying thus to think everything false, it was necessary that I, who was thinking this, was something. And observing that this truth '*I* [*think*], *therefore I* [*am*]' was so firm and sure that all the most extravagant suppositions of the sceptics were incapable of shaking it, I decided that I could accept it without scruple as the first principle of the philosophy I was seeking. (*Discourse,* Part IV; AT VI, 32; CSM I, 127)

> [A]m not I, at least, something? But I have just said that I have no senses and no body. This is the sticking point: what follows from this? Am I not so bound up with a body and with senses that I cannot exist without them? But I have convinced myself that there is absolutely nothing in the world, no sky, no earth, no minds, no bodies. Does it now follow that I too do not exist? No: if I convinced myself of something then I certainly existed. But there is a deceiver of supreme power and cunning who is deliberately and constantly deceiving me. In that case I too undoubtedly exist, if he is deceiving me; and let him deceive me as much as he can, he will never bring it about that I am nothing as long as I think that I am something. So after considering everything very thoroughly, I must finally conclude that this proposition, *I am, I exist,* is necessarily true whenever it is put forward by me or conceived in my mind. (Meditation II; AT VII, 25; CSM II, 16–17)

The literature on these two passages, which is simply enormous, testifies both to the ingenuity of interpreters and to the difficulty of pinning Descartes down. Despite the great range of options open to the reader, one can fairly say, I think, that there are three main lines of interpretation in the literature, (1) the single-intuition interpretation, (2) the inference interpretation, and (3) the performative interpretation.

According to the first option, one grasps the certainty of 'I think, therefore I am' in a single intuition. Descartes provides major support for this reading in the following passage from his Reply to Objection II: "When someone says 'I [think], therefore I am, or I exist', he does not deduce existence from thought by means of a syllogism, but recognizes it as something self-evident by a simple intuition of the mind" (AT VI, 140; CSM II, 100). One problem with this interpretation is understanding how, not just 'I am', but 'I think, therefore I am' can possibly be a single intuition, or, perhaps better put, what it could mean to say, as Descartes says, that one "recognizes it as something self-evident by a simple intuition of the mind." Perhaps the simple intuition is this: in thinking, I am. But it is hard to be clear about just what that intuition would be. For one thing, the logical form of 'in thinking, I am' is obscure.

In consequence of this problem, some commentators suppose that there are really two simple intuitions—'I think' and 'I am'—whereas others suppose that 'I think' is really superfluous and the simple intuition concerns only 'I am'. This last version of the single-intuition interpretation gains some plausibility, perhaps, from concentration on the formulation in Meditation II (*"I am, I exist,* is necessarily true whenever it is put forward by me or conceived in my mind") and also, as Kenny maintains, from Descartes's statement in the *Rules for the Direction of the Mind* that "everyone can mentally intuit that he exists" (AT X, 368; CSM I, 14).[2]

So, the first main interpretation, the single-intuition interpretation, splits into three: it may be taken full strength (the "simple" intuition is then the whole thought, 'I think, therefore I am') or else in either of two weaker versions (two simple intuitions, or just 'I am'). So much for the first main line of interpretation.

The second interpretation (the cogito as inference) rests heavily on Descartes's use, in the *Discourse* and elsewhere, though not in the *Meditations,* of the word *ergo* ('therefore'). But this interpretation also gains support from the many passages in which Descartes seems to talk about the cogito as an inference, as he does in the letter to Colvius quoted above, and also, for example, in this famous part of his reply to Gassendi, that is, to Objections V:

> I may not, for example, make the inference 'I [walk], therefore I exist', except in so far as the awareness of walking is a thought. The inference is certain only if applied to this awareness, and not to the movement of the body which sometimes—in the case of dreams—is not occurring at all, despite the fact that I seem to myself to be walking. Hence from the fact that I think I am walking I can very well infer the existence of a mind which has this thought, but not the existence of a body that walks. (AT VI, 352; CSM II, 244)

A prima facie difficulty for this interpretation is, for example, the Reply to Objections II (AT VI, 140; CSM II, 100), where Descartes insists that one who says, "I think, therefore I am," in fact "does not deduce existence from thought by means of a syllogism. . . ." Perhaps that comment should move us to distinguish two arguments. The first is this:

(1a)   Whatever thinks, is.
(2)   I think (that is, I am something that thinks).

Therefore,

(3)   I am.

This is the second:

(1b)   If I think, I am.
(2)   I think.

Therefore,

(3)   I am.

One might plausibly think of argument (1a–3) as a syllogism and yet deny that argument (1b–3) is syllogistic; the latter has the simple form of *modus ponens*.[3] One could add, as Descartes seems to suggest in various passages, that even if (1a) might be thought, in an important way, to underlie (1b), still (1b) has a kind of primacy of its own. Indeed, the continuation of the passage from the Reply to Objections II seems to suggest that thought:

> [If one] were deducing it by means of a syllogism, he would have to have had previous knowledge of the major premiss 'Everything which thinks is, or exists'; yet in fact he learns it from experiencing in his own case that it is impossible that he should think without existing. It is in the nature of our mind to construct general propositions on the basis of our knowledge of particular ones. (AT VII, 140–41; CSM II, 100)

Though the more plausible version of the inference interpretation, I think, would have Descartes presenting argument (1b–3), there are certainly some passages in which Descartes seems to admit that it is argument (1a–3) that underlies the cogito after all. Perhaps this passage from the *Conversation with Burman* is the strongest: "Before this inference, 'I think therefore I am', the major [premise] 'whatever thinks is' can be known; for it is in reality prior to my inference, and my inference depends on it. This is why the author says in the *Principles* that the major premise comes first, namely because implicitly it is always presupposed and prior."[4]

---

3. Compare Bernard Williams, *Descartes: The Project of Pure Enquiry* (Harmondsworth: Penguin, 1978), 87.
4. *Descartes' Conversation with Burman*, trans. John Cottingham (Oxford: Clarendon Press, 1976), 4.

There is yet another way in which the cogito may be taken as an inference; it may be considered an *immediate* inference, that is, an inference from a single premise, as follows:

(2)   I think.

Therefore,

(3)   I am.

In standard modern logic, $(\exists x)(x = a)$ follows from any statement in which a occurs. If we take 'I' in any given context to be an individual constant, then, it seems, we can reason validly,

(4)   If I think, I think (or, If I walk, I walk, etc.).

Therefore,

(3)   I am.

But an inference of this sort seems far removed from the kind of thing that interests Descartes. Thus, if the cogito is to be thought of as an immediate inference, the ground of its validity ought to be something other than the rule of existential generalization that get us from, say, (2) to (3).

Easily the most sophisticated effort to defend the immediate-inference interpretation is that offered by Jerrold J. Katz, who suggests that the cogito is an analytic entailment. It is not to be taken as a logically valid inference, or as an enthymeme for a logically valid inference; nevertheless it is, Katz insists, formally valid on purely semantic grounds, much as, he supposes, 'Descartes had a nightmare, hence Descartes had a dream' is formally, though not logically, valid.[5]

5. Jerrold J. Katz, *Cogitations* (New York: Oxford University Press, 1986), 25–26, 134. See also Katz, "Descartes's Cogito," *Pacific Philosophical Quarterly* 68 (1987), 175–96.

Since, as Katz himself maintains, his interpretation requires him to present and defend a "philosophy of logic and language which gives substance to the possibility that the standard conception of inference is wrong," it cannot be adequately evaluated here.[6] I content myself with remarking that, though this is a very attractive interpretation of 'cogito, ergo sum', it does not seem to fit the *Meditations* formulation, "*I am, I exist,* is necessarily true whenever it is put forward by me or conceived in my mind."[7]

Again our main line of interpretation has split into three. The cogito may be thought of as a syllogistic inference, an argument of the form *modus ponens,* or an immediate inference, especially, perhaps, as an analytic entailment. Of these three options, the idea of an analytic entailment is perhaps the most attractive, though it fits the *Discourse* better than the *Meditations.*

Finally, there is Jaakko Hintikka's performative interpretation. The key idea for this reading is the notion that *saying* or *thinking* "I exist" is self-warranting or self-verifying; that is, the very act of saying it or thinking it shows that what one says or thinks is true (much as saying or thinking "I am here" guarantees the truth of what is said or thought).[8] The plausibility of such an interpretation of Descartes rests heavily on the way the cogito is formulated in Meditation II (which is, we should note, repeated nowhere else in Descartes's corpus): "*I am, I exist* is necessarily true each time it is uttered by me or conceived mentally."

Each of these three main interpretations has something to be said in its favor. In particular, for each one there seems to be at least one passage in Descartes that favors it over the other two. The latest philosophy journal may bring yet a more polished and sophisticated version of this one or that; but

6. *Cogitations,* 131.
7. Katz suggests but does not develop a rather different approach to the *Meditations* formulation in his "Descartes's Cogito," 194.
8. Jaakko Hintikka, "*Cogito, Ergo Sum:* Inference or Performance?" *Philosophical Review* 71 (1962), 3–32.

each of these three is too well-grounded in Cartesian texts to be obliterated by an even more sophisticated version of one of its rivals.

In view of this exegetical impasse, I suggest that we adopt a different strategy. We should try looking for an overarching interpretation that preserves all the primary readings and makes clear why there are several interpretations of this central idea (or, perhaps, cluster of ideas) in Descartes's philosophy. An approach that does just that, I suggest, is what I call "the methodological interpretation." This interpretation seems to be a version of what Fred Feldman has called the "epistemic discovery" interpretation, and I find it also suggested by E. M. Curley.[9] But I may have read too much into Feldman or Curley, and I have no wish to add exegetical controversy concerning them to exegetical controversy concerning Descartes. So I present the methodological interpretation in my own way—with the acknowledgment that I find support in their commentaries. But first we need to do a little stage setting.

❧

The main project of the *Meditations* is something I refer to as the rational reconstruction of knowledge (see the Appendix). It is announced in the second sentence of Meditation I: "I realized that it was necessary, once in the course of my life, to demolish everything completely and start again right from the foundations if I wanted to establish anything at all in the sciences that was stable and likely to last" (AT VII, 17; CSM II, 12). The same idea seems to structure Part IV of the *Discourse* and Part I of the *Principles of Philosophy.*

To get started on the rational reconstruction of knowledge,

9. Fred Feldman, *A Cartesian Introduction to Philosophy* (New York: McGraw-Hill, 1986), chap. 4; E. M. Curley, *Descartes against the Skeptics* (Cambridge: Harvard University Press, 1978), 86.

Descartes adopts the method of systematic doubt (also called the method of hyperbolical doubt). Following that method, "I should hold back my assent from opinions which are not completely certain and indubitable just as carefully as I do from those which are patently false" (AT VII, 18; CSM II, 12). As he puts the matter in Part IV of the *Discourse,* "I thought it necessary to . . . reject as if absolutely false everything in which I could imagine the least doubt, in order to see if I was left believing anything that was entirely indubitable" (AT VI, 31; CSM I, 127).

The method of systematic doubt is not something Descartes defends against objections or tries to justify in any way. Perhaps he should be criticized for not seeking to justify his choice of this method. But perhaps one could answer on his behalf that no serious investigation can begin without assuming some methodological framework. To justify the method of systematic doubt one would have to presuppose some other methodological framework. One must begin somewhere. As he puts it in Rule IV, "it is far better never to contemplate investigating the truth about any matter than to do so without a method" (AT X, 371; CSM I, 16).

In any case, having adopted the method of systematic doubt, Descartes begins to consider candidates for certainty, that is, candidates for something he cannot reject as false because he cannot doubt it at all, on any grounds. Most of Meditation I is taken up with the consideration and rejection of such candidates. Finally, in Meditation II, Descartes considers his own existence. He realizes that he cannot succeed in doubting his own existence. For him 'I am, I exist' is immune to doubt. He thus accepts it as his first principle, as the foundation stone for his rational reconstruction of knowledge. Or, as he puts it in the parallel passage from the *Discourse,* Part IV, "observing that this truth '*I [think], therefore I [am]*' was so firm and sure that all the most extravagant suppositions of the sceptics were incapable of shaking it, I decided that I could accept it without scruple as the first principle of the philoso-

phy I was seeking" (AT VI, 32; CSM I, 127). By "the first
principle of the philosophy I was seeking" Descartes means, I
take it, the foundation stone in what I am calling "the rational
reconstruction of knowledge."

It is important to be clear about what is *not* happening here.
Descartes is not using the method of systematic doubt, or any
part of that method, as a premise in an argument for the
conclusion 'I exist', or for the conclusion '"I exist" is the first
principle of my philosophy', or for '"I think, therefore I am"
is the first principle of my philosophy'. Thus he is not, for
example, reasoning this way:

(5)   Whatever I cannot doubt is the case.
(6)   I cannot doubt that I exist.

Therefore,

(7)   I exist.

Rather, Descartes is *using* the method of systematic doubt to
test candidates for first principle and to select 'I am'.

Perhaps a good way to think of Descartes's procedure is to
imagine him adopting his method of systematic doubt and
then turning to a worksheet such as the one illustrated here.
After testing several candidates, he is able to enter "I am" as
the first principle. But it is important to see that no argument
with 'I am' as conclusion is part of the rational reconstruction
of knowledge. Furthermore, more than one noncompeting
reason may be entered in the worksheet to justify checking
"Cannot doubt" on the worksheet. Thus, and this is the most
important implication of the interpretation I am offering, the
ingenious efforts by commentators to find a single interpretation of the cogito (in the broad sense) that unifies Descartes's
various comments on its special status are misplaced. Since
those comments concern the conscientious application of the
method of systematic doubt and not directly the rational re-

Worksheet for the rational reconstruction of knowledge

Candidate for first principle	Can doubt	Cannot doubt	Reasons
What has been accepted from the senses	√		The senses sometimes mislead me, and it is prudent never to trust wholly those things that have once deceived us.
I am here seated by the fire (etc.)	√		I have been deceived in sleep, and there are no conclusive indications to distinguish waking life.
I am		√	(i) Since I persuaded myself of something, I was. (ii) If someone deceives me, I am. (iii) 'I exist' is necessarily true each time I utter or conceive it.

Instructions: When you enter something in the worksheet that warrants a check in the "Cannot doubt" column, enter that item below as the first principle in the rational reconstruction of knowledge.
FIRST PRINCIPLE: I am

construction of knowledge itself, there need be no presumption that Descartes should have restricted himself to a single reason for supposing that 'I am' cannot be doubted.

It is worth getting as clear as one can about what Descartes considers appropriate reasons for checking "Can doubt" and "Cannot doubt" on his worksheet. The reasons he offers for "can doubt that *p*" may be taken, indifferently, as (i) reasons for thinking it might be false that *p*, and (ii) reasons for thinking I might be deceived in thinking that *p*. Thus, 'I have been deceived in sleep and there are no conclusive indications for distinguishing waking life' might be taken either as (a) a reason for thinking it might be false that I am seated here by the fire, or (b) a reason for thinking I might be deceived in thinking that I am seated here by the fire.

Concerning reasons for checking "Cannot doubt" (which are crucial for understanding the cogito), the situation is very different. There are, I think, at least three different sorts of reason I might have for supposing that I cannot doubt that p: (i) reasons for supposing my belief that p is too firmly held for me to be able to doubt it; (ii) reasons for supposing that it could not be false that p; and (iii) reasons for supposing that I cannot be mistaken about whether p.

Descartes never shows any interest in sort (i) at all. In fact, it would not be appropriate for him to be interested in (i), given that his method of systematic doubt is meant to develop a reconstruction of knowledge that is rational. A prejudice might be so strongly held by him that it is completely unshakable—but that would hardly make it a good first principle for the rational reconstruction of knowledge.

What about (ii)? A natural place to find Descartes interested in this sort of reason for being unable to doubt something is in his consideration of '2 + 3 = 5'. When he rejects this as a first principle, he does so by asking, rhetorically, "How can I be sure but that God has brought it about that I am always mistaken when I add two and three?" (Meditation I). Clearly, that consideration bears not on whether it could be false that 2 + 3 = 5, but on whether one could be mistaken in thinking this.

Thus what Descartes seeks is not (ii) but (iii). A reason for entering one of my beliefs in the worksheet and checking the "Cannot doubt" column must be a reason for thinking, concerning that belief, that I cannot be mistaken about it. Even if the belief that 2 + 3 = 5 could not be false, one could still be mistaken about it; or at least that is what Descartes suggests in Meditation I. With 'I exist' the situation is quite otherwise. I cannot be mistaken about that. Realizing that I cannot be mistaken, I cannot doubt it.

What we should say, now, about the three different interpretations of the cogito is that they give us various reasons for thinking that I cannot be mistaken about whether I exist.

Accordingly, I cannot be mistaken because (i) I grasp 'I exist' or 'I think, therefore I am' as a single intuition; (ii) I see that 'I think, therefore I am' is an unimpeachable inference from unimpeachable premises; (iii) my uttering or conceiving 'I exist' shows that what is said or thought is true; and finally (to add a consideration important to Descartes, though it is not emphasized by any of the going interpretations) (iv) to be deceived, I would have to exist.

There is no reason at all why Descartes cannot have several reasons for checking "Cannot doubt" after 'I am'. My suggestion is that these points are not competing interpretations of the cogito or, anyway, are not best seen as such, but rather noncompeting reasons Descartes offers in various places for thinking that I cannot doubt that I am; that is, there are various reasons for thinking that I cannot be mistaken about whether I am.

Someone may object that my "Reasons" column simply reintroduces the old problem about how the cogito could possibly be rock bottom. Do the various reasons not introduce enthymematic arguments for the conclusion, 'I am'? And could one not ask for reasons to accept the premises of those arguments, as well as for reasons to consider the form of the arguments valid? Descartes does not want us to view the situation this way. He does not want us to think of these reasons as argumentative support for 'I am', but only as bona fides for the "Cannot doubt" check. They show only that one is serious about checking "Cannot doubt" and that one understands "Cannot doubt" in the relevant way.

èa

Finding a "first principle" that one cannot doubt is, as we have just seen, the first major task in Descartes's rational reconstruction of knowledge. It leads Descartes to ask

(8)   Can I doubt that I* exist?

an 'I*' question of great historical interest and importance.
Descartes does not even raise the question

(9)   Can I doubt that René Descartes exists?

If he had raised that question, he would have had to answer
"yes," even though

(10) I am René Descartes

is, for him, true enough, and he even believes it to be so. The
point is that (10), though true for him, is not for him indubitable.

  The distinction between (8) and (9) is important if we are to
understand just what Descartes has established as the foundation stone in his rational reconstruction of knowledge. Beyond that, it is important, as we see in the chapters to come, if
we are to understand what Descartes takes to be the nature of
the subject whose knowledge is being reconstructed and what
he thinks of as the natural parameters for that reconstruction.

[3]

The Augustinian Cogito

"How can I be mistaken [in thinking] that I[*] am?"
(*City of God*, XI.26). Augustine, not Descartes, seems to have
been the first thinker to ask this most famous of 'I*' questions.
Here is the complete passage in which he does so.

For we are, and we know that we are, and we love to be and to
know that we are. And in this trinity of being, knowledge, and
love there is not a shadow of illusion to disturb us. For we do not
reach these inner realities with our bodily senses as we do external objects, as, for example, color by seeing, sound by hearing,
odor by smelling, flavor by tasting, hard or soft objects by
touching. In the case of such sensible things, the best we can do
is to form very close and immaterial images which help us to
turn them over in our minds, to hold them in our memory, and
thus to keep our love for them alive. But without any illusion of
image, fancy, or phantasm, I am certain that I am, that I know
that I am, and that I love to be and to know.

In the face of these truths, the quibbles of the skeptics lose
their force. If they say, 'What if you are mistaken?'—well, if I
am mistaken, I am. For if one does not exist, he can by no
means be mistaken. Therefore, I am, if I am mistaken. Because,
therefore, I am, if I am mistaken, *how can I be mistaken [in think-
ing] that I am,* since it is certain that I am, if I am mistaken. And
because, if I could be mistaken, I would have to be the one who
is mistaken, therefore, I am most certainly not mistaken in

knowing that I am. Nor, as a consequence, am I mistaken in knowing that I know. For, just as I know that I am, I also know that I know. And when I love both to be and to know, then I add to the things I know a third and equally important knowledge, the fact that I love. (*City of God*, XI.26)

Though this passage is certainly famous, it has received much less critical scrutiny than the cogito passages in Descartes. Augustine had no Arnauld or Gassendi to question him or force him to elaborate or clarify his position. And there are no traditions for interpreting his 'si fallor, sum' ('If I am mistaken, I am') comparable to the traditions for interpreting Descartes's cogito.

Here is Jaakko Hintikka's assessment of Augustine:

In so far as I know, there is no indication that Augustine was ever alive to the possibility of interpreting his version of the *Cogito* as a performance rather than as an inference or as a factual observation. As far as Augustine is concerned, it would be quite difficult to disprove a "logical" interpretation such as Gassendi and others have given of the Cartesian *cogito* argument. What he dwells on is merely the "impossibility of thinking without existing." I do not see any way in which Augustine could have denied that *ambulo, ergo sum* or *video, ergo sum* are as good inferences as cogito, *ergo sum* and the sole difference between them lies in the different degree of certainty of their premises.[1]

With the claim that Augustine is not alive to the idea of a performative cogito I agree completely. Hintikka suggests that that leaves two possible interpretations of Augustine, a logical one and a factual one. I am not clear as to what the factual one might be; Hintikka does not elaborate. The logical

---

1. "*Cogito, Ergo Sum:* Inference or Performance?" *Philosophical Review* 71 (1962), 3-32, quotation from p. 23.

interpretation is, I take it, what we might call the "particular," or *modus ponens,* version of the inferential interpretation,

(1)   If I think, I am.
(2)   I think.

Thus,

(3)   I am.

together with the assurance that the first premise, being an instance of the provable formula $B(a) \rightarrow (\exists x)(x = a)$, is logically true.

This is very puzzling. Surely Augustine is not to be taken as offering this *modus ponens* argument:

(4)   If I am mistaken, I am.
(5)   I am mistaken.

Thus,

(6)   I am.

What then?

Perhaps for the logical interpretation of Augustine Hintikka has in mind a constructive dilemma similar to the following argument, which Hintikka presents in connection with his discussion of Descartes:

(7)   If Homer is a Greek, he exists.
(8)   If Homer is a barbarian, he exists.
(9)   Either Homer is a Greek or Homer is a barbarian.

Thus,

(10) He exists.

The analogue would go this way:

(11) If I am mistaken, I am.
(12) If I am not mistaken, I am.
(13) Either I am mistaken or I am not mistaken.

Thus,

(14) I am.

The parallel is not exact. The support for (11) has to be very different from that for (12). Indeed, for them both to be true, there must be a shift in the way the antecedent is taken:

(11′) If I am mistaken (about anything whatsoever), I am.
(12′) If I am not mistaken (in thinking that I am), I am.

On this reading, for the argument to be valid, (13) must be taken, not as a truism, but rather as this:

(13′) Either I am mistaken (about something—anything will do) or I am not mistaken (in thinking that I am).

Augustine might indeed have offered an argument that rests for its plausibility on an equivocation. So this criticism of the argument is not by itself sufficient reason for rejecting it as a reconstruction of Augustine. The main trouble with it as a reconstruction is that it yields the conclusion 'I am', whereas the conclusion Augustine seems to get is rather 'I know that I am'.

In "*Si Fallor, Sum,*" I suggested a reading of this passage according to which Augustine's aim is, not to establish 'I exist' as the conclusion of a sound argument, but rather to under-mine a threat to his claim to know that he exists.[2] According

2. In *Augustine: A Collection of Critical Essays,* ed. R. A. Markus (Garden City, N.Y.: Anchor Books, 1972), 151–67.

to that reading, Augustine supposes that one knows immediately and directly that one exists. But then one may wish to
take note of skepticism. The Academic, or skeptic, makes it a
life work to call knowledge claims into question. Augustine
gives the skeptic full play. In many cases, he agrees, the skeptic's taunt, "You might be mistaken," is effective; but not in
this one. When I say, "I know that I am," and the skeptic
taunts me, I can turn the taunt aside. "If I am mistaken," I
can reply, "I am." My reply is not part of an effort to establish
my existence, or my knowledge of my existence, by a proof;
rather, it has the negative aim of defeating a challenge to my
claim to know that I exist.

I still think that that analysis is correct. But it now occurs to
me that I can provide a reconstruction of the text that is more
satisfying and leads to the same moral. We begin with this
premise:

(15) Either I know that I am or I am mistaken in thinking
      that I am.

Suppose, for reduction to absurdity,

(16) I am mistaken in thinking that I am.

So

(17) I am mistaken. (from 16)
(18) If I am mistaken, I am. (additional premise)

So

(19) I am. (from 17 and 18 by *modus ponens*)
(20) If I am, I am not mistaken in thinking that I am.
      (tautology)

So

(21) I am not mistaken in thinking that I am. (from 19 and
      20 by *modus ponens*)

We can now discharge supposition (16), which has been shown
to lead to self-contradiction, and simply conclude

(21) I am not mistaken in thinking that I am.

But, by disjunctive syllogism, (21) and our original (15) yield

(22) I know that I am.

This is quite a successful reconstruction of the reasoning in
the text, I think. But it raises in dramatic form the question,
why did Augustine assume premise (15)? Why did he assume
that there are just these two alternatives: (i) I know that I am,
and (ii) I am mistaken in thinking that I am? Why did not he
consider, for example, the possibility that I am right in thinking that I am, but without knowing it?

As I have already suggested, the answer seems to be that
Augustine considers his knowledge that he exists direct and
paradigmatic knowledge. He sees no need to justify the claim
to that knowledge by appeal to anything that might be considered more basic than it. Still, he wants to respond to the
taunts of the Academic skeptics. So he is concessive. "Either I
am right," he says in effect, "or you are right; that is, either I
know that I exist, or, as you say, I am mistaken in thinking that
I exist." From that concession, he proves that he knows that
he exists.

২৯

What can we learn from this discussion about the role of 'I
am' in the philosophies of Augustine and Descartes? Skepticism plays an important role in the thinking of both philoso-

phers. To Augustine, skepticism is an important threat; but
what is threatening is, so to speak, global, or universal,
skepticism—being skeptical about everything. To put the matter another way, what is threatening is skepticism as a way of
life.

In Book V of his *Confessions*, Augustine recounts something
of the struggle he went through as he came to find Manichea-
nism unsatisfactory but had not yet become a Christian con-
vert. There seems to have been a brief period, when he was
about thirty, when he found Academic skepticism attractive as
a life orientation: "I began to think that the philosophers
known as Academics were wiser than the rest, because they
held that everything was a matter of doubt and asserted that
man can know nothing for certain" (V.10). Now, clearly there
is a problem with claiming to know for certain that

(23) Nothing can be known for certain.

If (23) is true, then it itself cannot be known for certain.

In *Against the Academics*, Augustine presents almost the re-
verse difficulty. The Academics, he says, claim to know that
nothing can be known. They base their claim on a criterion
for knowledge put forward by Zeno the Stoic. But if they
know that criterion, Augustine urges, they know something,
and so they are wrong in making their claim that nothing can
be known (III.9.18).

Yet, Augustine also seems to realize that the acceptability of
global skepticism need not rest on whether one can defend
(23) successfully as a *knowledge* claim; rather, the acceptability
of global skepticism could be demonstrated by the success of a
skeptic at challenging all putative knowledge claims. And so
Augustine sets out to deny the skeptic success by making the
knowledge claim

(22) I know that I* am.

Against (22) the skeptic is impotent. Thus, in the passage above from the *City of God*, Augustine begins with (22). Against that, he argues, the skeptical "What if you are mistaken?" is futile.

Augustine claims to know much else besides the fact that he* exists. In the same passage he also claims to know that he* loves to be. And among the knowledge claims he puts forward in *Against the Academics* (III.10.23–11.26) are these:

(24) There is one world or not.

(25) If there is not (only) one world, then the number of worlds is finite or infinite.

(26) This world is ordered either by the intrinsic nature of corporeal matter or by some providence.

(27) The world either always was and always will be, or began to be and will never cease to be, or began to be and will cease.

(28) Understanding by 'world' what now appears to me, the world exists.

(29) If there are one and six worlds, there are seven worlds.

(30) Three times three is nine.

(31) Something looks white to me (sounds delightful to me, smells sweet to me, tastes pleasant to me).

According to Augustine's general position, however, knowledge and understanding, especially about "deep and hidden things," presuppose belief (more on this in Chapter 11). He simply has no project, as Descartes does, of providing, on its own foundations, a rational reconstruction of knowledge.

Descartes uses skepticism to provide an independent foundation for reconstructing knowledge. Having adopted the method of systematic doubt, I can, according to Descartes, take the failure of the skeptic to call my existence successfully into question as a certification of 'I am' (or 'I think, therefore

I am') as my first principle. In Descartes it is not just that skepticism undermines itself and so discredits itself; nor is it that skepticism must break down somewhere. It is rather that skepticism can itself be used, methodologically, in reconstructing knowledge. Descartes turns a defensive action into an offensive tactic in the battle to acquire, or at least reconstruct, knowledge.

≈

Can it be that 'I am' is for Augustine nothing more than part of his favorite means of discrediting Academic skepticism? That seems unduly dismissive. Charles Taylor thinks that there is much more to 'I am' in Augustine than this. He writes, "Augustine was the inventor of the argument we know as the 'cogito', because Augustine was the first to make the first-person standpoint fundamental to our search for truth."[3] Suppose that that is right. What does it mean? What could it mean "to make the first-person standpoint fundamental to our search for truth"—if not to reconstruct knowledge from a first-person point of view in the fashion of Descartes?

Augustine is certainly preoccupied with the inward search for truth. "Do not go abroad," he writes in a famous passage in *Of True Religion*. "Return within yourself. In the inward man dwells truth" (39.72).[4] Indeed, Augustine suggests again and again that what I can know is to be found "in me." But what could it mean to say that what I can know is to be found in me? Augustine seems to suppose that items of each of the following sorts are to be found "within": (i) truths about my existence that are transparent to me (including the truth that

3. *Sources of the Self* (Cambridge: Harvard University Press, 1989), 113.
4. For other passages in which Augustine encourages himself, or others, to look inward, see *Against the Academics*, III.19.42; *On the Greatness of the Soul*, 28.55; *On Free Choice of the Will*, II.16.41.

I exist, that I know I exist, and that I love to exist)[5]; (ii) what *seems* to me to be so (as in 31 above); and (iii) simple a priori truths (as in 24–30 above). But, for Augustine, the search for truth should include much more than a search for items of these sorts. According to him, I need most of all to search out the truths of God as found in the Bible. To appropriate these truths I need to understand them. It is not enough to believe them in an "external" way, for example, by believing that what Moses (or whoever the author of Genesis was) wrote in Genesis 1:1 is true (whatever it should turn out to mean). I need to be able to interpret that verse for myself. And this Augustine thinks of as finding its truth within oneself. In this way, then, Augustine makes the first-person standpoint "fundamental to our search for truth." This is a subject to which we return in Chapters 12 and 13. As I indicated in the previous chapter, Augustine anticipates Descartes, not only in presenting cogito-like reasoning, but also in developing reasoning about the *nature* of the mind that is revealed to exist by that cogito-type reasoning. Just how that reasoning goes is the subject of Chapter 4.

5. The cogito-like passage in the *Trinity* uses 'I live' instead of 'I am' for the sample truth immune to the taunts of the skeptics. Augustine then tries to build up from this simple truth an infinite number of similarly invulnerable truths by the iteration of 'I know': "For he who says: 'I know that I live,' says that he knows one thing; if he were then to say: 'I know that I know that I live,' there are already two things, but that he knows these two, is to know a third thing; and so he can add a fourth and a fifth, and innumerable more, as long as he is able to do so. But because he cannot comprehend an innumerable number by adding one thing to another, or express a thing innumerable times, he comprehends this very fact and says with absolute certainty that this is both true and so innumerable that he cannot truly comprehend and express its infinite number" (XV.12.21).

[4]

My Mind and I

The idea that thoughts are private to the thinker, as well as the idea that one can know what one thinks without knowing anything about the neurophysiological basis for that thought, are claims familiar to readers of modern philosophy. But one would be hard pressed to find any clear statement of these two ideas in ancient philosophy. Perhaps they find their earliest clear expression in the writings of Augustine, as in this passage: "[A]lthough we are said to think in our heart, and although we know what our thoughts are, without the knowledge of any other person, yet we know not in what part of the body we have the heart itself, where we do our thinking, unless we are taught it by some other person, who yet is ignorant of what we think" (*On the Soul and Its Origin,* IV.6.7). Augustine also develops the idea of a thinker who thinks these private thoughts. The most interesting passage in which he does so begins this way:

> [W]ho would doubt that he lives, remembers, understands, wills, thinks, knows, and judges? For even if he doubts, he lives; if he doubts, he remembers why he doubts; if he doubts, he understands that he doubts; if he doubts, he wishes to be certain; if he doubts, he thinks; if he doubts, he knows that he does not know; if he doubts, he judges that he ought not to consent rashly. Whoever then doubts about anything else ought never to

doubt about all of these; for if they were not, he would be unable to doubt about anything at all. (*Trinity,* X.10.14)

Prominent in these reflections is the idea that thoughts are fully transparent to the thinker who has them. Augustine follows these reflections with a paragraph devoted to the criticism of philosophers who suppose that the mind is a bodily substance or a disposition of some bodily substance. Augustine attempts to refute such materialists this way:

> All these [philosophers] overlook the fact that the mind [*mens*] knows itself, even when it seeks itself, . . . But we can in no way rightly say that anything is known while its substance [*substantia*] is unknown. Wherefore, since the mind knows itself, it knows its own substance. But it is certain about itself, as is clearly shown from what we have already said. But it is by no means certain whether it is air, or fire, or a body, or anything of a body. It is, therefore, none of these things. (*Trinity,* X.10.16)

The core of Augustine's argument here seems to be something like this:

(1)   If *x* knows *y,* then *x* knows the substance of *y.*
(2)   If *x* knows the substance of *y,* then for any stuff *z,* if *y* is *z,* then *x* is certain whether *y* is *z.*
(3)   The mind knows itself.

Therefore,

(4)   The mind knows its substance.

Therefore,

(5)   For any stuff *z,* if the mind is *z,* then the mind is certain whether it is *z.*

But

(6)   The mind is not certain whether it is air (or fire, or a body).

Therefore,

(7)   The mind is not air (or fire, or a body).

Augustine's question here is, 'What is the mind?' But his way of answering that question leads through the reasoning above to the related 'it*' question, 'What can the mind know, or be certain, that it* is?' Routing the question, 'What is the mind?' through the 'it*' question, 'What can the mind be certain that it* is?' turns out to be crucial to Augustine's reasoning and to its outcome. Since the mind knows itself, he reasons, it knows its own substance and thereby knows that it* is nothing material, but rather something that "lives, remembers, understand, wills, thinks and judges." It is, in the phrase Descartes later makes famous, "a thinking thing."

Augustine's list of mental functions is unsurprising to us post-Cartesians, except for the first item: "lives." According to Descartes, it is only by a confusion over whether an *anima* (soul) is a mind or, alternatively, an animator that one could think the mind has anything essential to do with living. Here is a revealing comment on that point from Descartes's Reply to Objections V:

> [P]rimitive man probably did not distinguish between, on the one hand, the principle by which we are nourished and grow and accomplish without any thought all the other operations which we have in common with the brutes, and, on the other hand, the principle in virtue of which we think. He therefore used the single term 'soul' to apply to both; and when he subsequently noticed that thought was distinct from nutrition, he called the element which thinks 'mind', and believed it to be the

principal part of the soul. I, by contrast, realizing that the principle by which we are nourished is wholly different—different
in kind—from that in virtue of which we think, have said that
the term 'soul', when it is used to refer to both these principles,
is ambiguous. If we are to take 'soul' in its special sense, as
meaning the 'first actuality' or 'principle of man', then the term
must be understood to apply only to the principle in virtue of
which we think; and to avoid ambiguity I have as far as possible
used the term 'mind' for this. For I consider the mind not as a
part of the soul but as the thinking soul in its entirety. (AT VII,
356; CSM II, 246)[1]

As we noted in the previous chapter, Augustine's cogito-like
reasoning sometimes incorporates 'I live' in place of 'I am' or
'I exist'. His use of 'live' and 'life' in such contexts seems to be
rather like the use preserved in modern English in the familiar question, 'Is there life after death?'—which does not
mean, 'Is there organic life after death?' but rather something
more like, 'Will we survive our deaths?' 'Will we continue to
exist after our deaths?' With this modern usage in mind, I
suggest that we understand 'lives' in Augustine to mean 'exists'. If we do so, Augustine's list of mental functions turns out
to be very, very Cartesian.

ঽৰ

In Descartes we find reasoning that is instructively both
similar to Augustine's and also different from it. Right after
hitting on the cogito, Descartes admits: "I do not yet have a

1. The idea that the (rational) soul is the animator of a human body is also
rejected in Articles 5 and 6 of Part 1 of Descartes's *Passions of the Soul*, in these
lines: "The error consists in supposing that since dead bodies are devoid of
heat and movement, it is the absence of the soul which causes this cessation of
movement and heat. . . . So as to avoid this error, let us note that death never
occurs through the absence of the soul, but only because one of the principal
parts of the body decays" (AT XI, 330; CSM I, 329). For more on this point,
and on its importance, see Gareth B. Matthews, "Consciousness and Life,"
Philosophy 52 (1977), 13–26.

sufficient understanding of what this 'I' is, that now necessarily exists." He resolves to go back and meditate on what he originally believed himself to be. He asks, "What did I originally believe that I[*] am?" Or, as he puts it a few lines later, "What then did I formerly think I[*] was?" (AT VII, 25; CSM II, 17).

As we saw earlier, Augustine, in his reasoning, helps himself to the premises 'If x knows y, then x knows the substance of y', and 'If x knows the substance of y, then for any stuff z, if y is z, then x is certain whether y is z'. Descartes's approach to these matters in Meditation II is remarkably different. He begins rather boldly. After announcing that he is a thinking thing, he adds this: "What else am I? I will use my imagination. I am not that structure of limbs which is called a human body. I am not even some thin vapour which permeates the limbs—a wind, fire, air, breath, or whatever I depict in my imagination; for these are things which I have supposed to be nothing. Let this supposition stand; for all that, I am still something" (AT VII, 27; CSM II, 18).[2] It looks as though the argument being presented here is this:

(8)   I can suppose that no bodies exist.
(9)   I cannot suppose that I do not exist.

Therefore,

(10) I am not a body.

---

2. Augustine, too, has an interesting argument from the imagination for concluding that the mind is not anything corporeal. But it is different from Descartes's argument. Augustine first claims that the mind must use a mental image to think of fire, air, or, in general, a body. But if the mind were any one of these, he continues, "it would not think [of] it through an imaginary phantasy, as absent things or something of the same kind which have been touched by the sense of the body are thought, but it would think it by a kind of inward presence, not feigned but real—for there is nothing more present to it than itself; just as it thinks that it lives, and remembers, and understands, and wills" (Trinity, X.10.16).

Certainly the reasoning from (8) and (9) to (10) is not an impressive argument. It is hardly better than this one:

(11) I can suppose that no children of Reka Matthews exist.

(12) I cannot suppose that I do not exist.

Therefore,

(13) I am not a child of Reka Matthews.

All that follows from (11) and (12) is

(13′) I can suppose that I am not a child of Reka Matthews.

Similarly, all that follows from (8) and (9) is

(10′) I can suppose that I am not a body.

Descartes seems to realize that his reasoning in this passage is not very impressive; he adds this comment: "And yet may it not perhaps be the case that these very things which I am supposing to be nothing, because they are unknown to me, are in reality identical with the 'I' of which I am aware?" That objection is precisely on target. Although Descartes is currently supposing, at this point in his reasoning, that perhaps nothing corporeal exists, that supposition does not rule out the possibility that, in fact, counter to his supposition, he is identical with some corporeal thing; that is, merely supposing that there are no bodies fails to provide any guarantee that, in fact, he is not a body.

Here is how Descartes responds to his own objection:

> I do not know, and for the moment I shall not argue the point, since I can make judgements only about things which are known to me. I know that I exist; the question is, what is this 'I'

that I know? If the 'I' is understood strictly as we have been taking it, then it is quite certain that knowledge of it does not depend on things of whose existence I am as yet unaware; so it cannot depend on any of the things which I invent in my imagination. (AT VII, 27–28; CSM II, 18–19)

Descartes's talk here of "this 'I' that I know [to exist]" (*ego ille quem novi [existere]*) is instructive.[3] This 'I', if, as Descartes puts it, it is "understood strictly, as we have been taking it" is, so to speak, what is referred to by Descartes's use of 'I*'. It is what is known to him when he knows this: "I exist." It is his thought's ego.

Descartes makes specific references to what I am calling his thought's ego throughout Meditation II. Here are some of them:

So I must be on my guard against carelessly taking something else to be this 'I', and so making a mistake in the very item of knowledge that I maintain is the most certain and evident of all. (AT VII, 25; CSM II, 18)

Is it not one and the same 'I' who is now doubting almost everything, who nonetheless understands some things, who affirms that this one thing is true, denies everything else, desires to

3. Anthony Kenny thinks that Descartes equivocates on the expression *ego quem novi*. It may mean, he thinks, 'I, who am known by me' or 'I, qua known by me'. "The first time it is used in this passage," Kenny writes, "it must be taken in the former sense. The I, who is known by me to be a *res cogitans,* may also be, for all I know, a body. The second time it is used it must be taken in the latter sense. The I, qua known by me to be a *res cogitans,* is not more than that"; *Descartes: A Study of His Philosophy* 88. But Descartes himself adds, after using the expression the second time, "If the 'I' is understood strictly [*praecise sumpti*]," which suggests that he is onto Kenny's worry, indeed that he first allows something rather like Kenny's first interpretation and then insists on something more like the second. It is doubtless relevant that Kenny himself translates *huius sic praecise sumpti notitiam* as "the knowledge of this I so qualified." CSM's "understood strictly," or "understood thus strictly," without the addition "as we have been taking it," is perhaps preferable.

know more, is unwilling to be deceived. . . . (AT VII, 28; CSM II, 19)

But it still appears—and I cannot stop thinking this—that the corporeal things of which images are formed in my thought, and which the senses investigate, are known with much more distinctness than this puzzling 'I' which cannot be pictured in the imagination. (AT VII, 29; CSM II, 20)

What exactly is "this puzzling 'I'"? What is Descartes's thought's ego? Or what, anyway, does Descartes take it to be? It is *something with all and only those features Descartes knows himself* to have simply in virtue of knowing that he* exists.* It certainly excludes contingent truths about the man, Descartes— for example, truths about where and when he was born, about what places he has visited, where he has been schooled, and so forth. He can know that he* exists without knowing that these items are true of him*. But it also excludes even his having, or being, a body.

From our contemporary point of view, a natural thing to say about this discussion is that it trades on the referential opacity of the 'I*' position. At this point in his deliberations, Descartes has neither established nor ruled out the possibility that there are bodies. He can, he indicates, entertain the possibility that he is a body: ". . . may it not perhaps be the case that these very [corporeal] things which I am supposing to be nothing, because they are unknown to me, are in reality identical with the 'I' of which I am aware?" Thus, Descartes entertains this possibility:

(14) I am something corporeal.

Suppose, he goes on, (14) is true and, moreover,

(15) I know that I* exist.

Does this follow?

(16) I know that something corporeal exists.

Not at all. Even on the supposition that I am in fact something corporeal, it does not follow from 'I know that I exist' that I *know* that I am something corporeal. The 'I*' position is not, as we should say today, open to substitution.

What this discussion suggests is that I may assign to thought's ego all and only those features $f_1, f_2, \ldots$ such that from

(15) I know that I* exist

this follows:

(17) I know that something with features $f_1, f_2, \ldots$ exists.

According to Descartes, the relevant features are precisely the features of a *res cogitans,* a thinking thing—no more and no less.

What Descartes proposes early on in Meditation II, and thinks he has established by the end, is that he* is (at least) a thinking thing. This is all he thinks that he has established. He does not suppose that he has established that he* is *not* a corporeal thing; the task of proving that is left for Meditation VI, where we find this reasoning:

> I know that everything which I clearly and distinctly under-
> stand is capable of being created by God so as to correspond
> exactly with my understanding of it. Hence the fact that I can
> clearly and distinctly understand one thing apart from another
> is enough to make me certain that the two things are distinct,
> since they are capable of being separated, at least by God. . . .
> [O]n the one hand I have a clear and distinct idea of myself, in

so far as I am simply a thinking, non-extended thing; and on the other hand I have a distinct idea of body, in so far as this is simply an extended, non-thinking thing. And accordingly, it is certain that I am really distinct from my body, and can exist without it. (AT VII, 78; CSM II, 54)

The core of Descartes's argument here seems to be this:

(18) If I can clearly and distinctly understand x apart from y, then x and y are capable of being separated by God.
(19) I can clearly and distinctly understand myself[*] apart from my body.

Therefore,

(20) My body and I are capable of being separated by God.
(21) If x and y are capable of being separated by God, then x and y are really distinct.

Therefore,

(22) My body and I are really distinct.

On my reconstruction, Descartes takes himself to have established (19) in Meditation II. It is established, he thinks, by pinning down the characteristics of my thought's ego, that is, by isolating those features I must know I have simply in knowing that I* exist. Those features turn out to be the features of a "thinking thing." The proof that those features characterize a substance distinct from my body, however, is left for Meditation VI. That proof is given in the reasoning from (18) through (22).

ટ▲

In both Augustine and Descartes there is an interesting development of the concept of mind and of the relation between mind and ego. Augustine presents the idea that thoughts are private to the thinker and the companion idea that thoughts are only uncertainly related to anything the thinker might suppose to be their physiological basis. He also develops an answer to the question, 'What is a mind?' by reasoning that leads through the question, 'What can the mind know, or be certain, that it* is?' Yet he fails, in these passages, actually to identify mind and ego.

Augustine could easily have reasoned in the following way (and here I am simply altering the passage from the *Trinity* that I quoted above by substituting 'I' for 'the mind'): "Wherefore, since I know myself, I know my own substance. But I am certain about myself, as is clearly shown from what we have already said. But I am by no means certain whether I am air, or fire, or a body, or anything of a body. I am, therefore, none of these things." I say Augustine *could* easily have reasoned in this way, but he does not. Moreover, it is an important fact about Augustine, and a crucial difference between him and Descartes, that he does not reason in this way.

Why does Augustine not reason in this way? Perhaps it is that, since he has always thought of himself as a rational soul *in a body*, it never occurs to him to identify himself, in this life anyway, with his own thought's ego—with what he knows to exist just in knowing this: "I exist." Instead, Augustine's view seems to be that in this life he is a soul or mind in a physical body, and in the life to come he is a mind or soul in the likeness of a physical body (see *The Literal Meaning of Genesis*, XII.32.60).

It is Descartes who attempts to answer the question, 'What am I?' (cf. 'What is the mind?') by reasoning that leads through the question, 'What can I know, or be certain, that I* am?' His answer to both questions is 'a mind', where, however, it must be added that what he takes a mind to be is something strikingly Augustinian.

ﾎ

It is a simplification, but not, I think, an oversimplification, to say that mind-body dualism arises in Augustine when he transforms the question, 'What is a mind?' into the 'it*' question, 'What can a mind know, or be certain, that it* is?' Similarly, mind-body dualism arises in Descartes when he transforms the question, 'What am I?' into the 'I*' question, 'What can I know, or be certain, that I* am?' I do not mean to suggest, however, that giving emphasis to this 'I*' question, or to its related 'it*' question, leads one inevitably to mind-body dualism. To get the conclusion that the mind is not air or fire or a body, Augustine uses the additional premises, 'If x knows y, then x knows the substance of y', and 'if x knows the substance of y, then for any stuff z, if y is z, then x is certain whether y is z'. One could certainly give prominence to the question, 'What can a mind be certain that it* is?' without being committed to those additional premises.[4]

Descartes uses several strong premises to establish "the real distinction" between mind and body: 'If I can clearly and distinctly understand x apart from y, then x and y are capable of being separated by God'; 'If x and y are capable of being separated by God, then x and y are really distinct'; and, perhaps most problematic, 'I can clearly and distinctly understand myself* apart from my body'. One could give prominence to the question, 'What can I be certain that I* am?' without accepting any such premises as those. Yet prolonged reflection on the certainty I have that I* exist at least invites me to think about what I can be certain that I* am. On discov-

4. Compare G. E. M. Anscombe's treatment of some of these same themes in "The First Person."

ery that the features I can be certain I* have do not include any corporeal features, I may be inspired to cast about for a set of premises by which I can prove that I* am an entity distinct from my body. Augustine comes remarkably close to doing just that. Descartes goes the whole way.

The difference between Augustine and Descartes in this matter deserves as much emphasis as does their similarity. The difference means that, for Augustine, the question, 'What can I be certain that I* am?' does not belong to the cluster of 'I*' questions that structure his philosophical perspective. He never considers that he* himself, right now, in this life, might simply *be* a mind, a thinking thing; rather, he assumes that, in this life, he is an embodied soul. In doing that, he, like everyone else before Descartes, assumes that there exist bodies.[5] Thus, as far as we can tell, he never thinks the thought that there might be no bodies at all, or even the thought that one should be able to say how one knows that there exist bodies. It is, apparently, Descartes who first thinks those thoughts. I discuss the way he confronts them in Chapter 6. But first we must take up another 'I*' question, one that Augustine asks quite as clearly and as insistently as Descartes does. That question is the subject of the next chapter.

5. On this point I agree with M. F. Burnyeat; see his "Idealism and Greek Philosophy: What Descartes Saw and Berkeley Missed," *Philosophical Review* 91 (1982), 3–40.

[5]

The Epistemological Dream Problem

After announcing his project for developing a rational reconstruction of knowledge back at the beginning of Meditation I, and after stating the method of systematic doubt, Descartes turns to applying the method so as to begin the reconstruction. Among the candidates for *indubitabilia* that he considers right away are these:

(1) I am here, sitting by the fire, wearing a winter dressing-gown, holding this piece of paper in my hands, etc.

(2) These hands and this whole body are mine.

Neither (1) nor (2) seems momentous enough to serve as a first principle in the rational reconstruction of knowledge. But if either should prove indubitable, it might warrant

(3) There are bodies,

which looks altogether more impressive. It is precisely at this point that Descartes introduces the dream hypothesis:

> How often, asleep at night, am I convinced of just such familiar events—that I am here in my dressing-gown, sitting by the

fire—when in fact I am lying undressed in bed! Yet at the moment my eyes are certainly wide awake when I look at this piece of paper; I shake my head and it is not asleep; as I stretch out and feel my hand I do so deliberately, and I know what I am doing. All this would not happen with such distinctness to someone asleep. Indeed! As if I did not remember other occasions when I have been tricked by exactly similar thoughts while asleep! As I think about this more carefully, I see plainly that there are never any sure signs by means of which being awake can be distinguished from being asleep. The result is that I begin to feel dazed, and this very feeling only reinforces the notion that I may be asleep. (AT VII, 19; CSM II, 13)

Although this passage has about it a remarkable vividness and great persuasive power, it did not please or impress all Descartes's contemporaries. Hobbes, in particular, was quite unimpressed. In his characteristically crotchety style he charges Descartes with peddling stale fish: "From what is said [in Meditation I]," Hobbes writes,

it is clear enough that there is no criterion enabling us to distinguish our dreams from the waking state and from veridical sensations. And hence the images we have when we are awake and having sensations are not accidents that inhere in external objects, and are no proof that any external objects exist at all. So if we follow our senses, without exercising our reason in any way, we shall be justified in doubting whether anything exists. I acknowledge the correctness of this Meditation. But since Plato and other ancient philosophers discussed this uncertainty in the objects of the senses, and since the difficulty of distinguishing the waking state from dreams is commonly pointed out, I am sorry that the author, who is so outstanding in the field of original speculations, should be publishing this ancient material. (Objections III; AT VII, 171; CSM II, 121)

There is some justice in Hobbes's complaint. What is sometimes called Descartes's dream problem ('How do I know that I* am not now dreaming?') could quite appropriately be called Plato's dream problem instead. Certainly it is presented clearly enough in this passage from Plato's *Theaetetus:*

> SOCRATES. Well, and there is one dispute . . . about sleeping and waking, which you can surely call to mind, can't you?
>
> THEAETETUS. What sort of dispute?
>
> SOCRATES. Something I imagine you've often heard people asking: What evidence one would be able to point to, if someone asked at this very moment whether we're asleep and dreaming everything that we have in mind, or awake and having a waking discussion with each other.
>
> THEAETETUS. Yes, Socrates, it certainly is difficult to see what evidence one could use to prove it; because all the features of the two states correspond exactly, like counterparts. The discussion we've just had could equally well have been one that we seemed, in our sleep, to be having with each other; and when, in a dream, we seem to be telling dreams, the similarity between the two sets of occurrences is extraordinary. (158bc)

This dream problem (let us call it the "epistemological dream problem") is found in Augustine, too. It may have reached him through Cicero (*Academica,* II.27.88ff.), whom we know Augustine read assiduously and whose ideas Augustine tried to come to terms with in his earliest extant treatise, the dialogue *Against the Academics.*

Augustine offers no solution to this dream problem. Instead, he proceeds concessively by granting that, as far as one knows, one may be asleep. He then tries to show that neither the certainty of various a priori truths nor his knowledge that he exists, that he lives, that he is enjoying a pleasant taste, and so forth is threatened by the taunt, "You may be dreaming." Here is one of several passages along that line: "Who would be so impertinent as to say to me as I savour with delight the taste of something: 'Perhaps there is nothing to taste; you are only dreaming'? Do I stop my savouring? No! I reply that even though I were dreaming, it would still delight me" (*Against the Academics*, III.11.26).

Augustine uses the same strategy in his mature writings. Here is the relevant part of the cogito-like passage from the *Trinity:*

> It is an inner knowledge by which we know that we live, where not even the Academician can say: "Perhaps you are sleeping, and you do not know, and you see in dreams." For who does not know that things seen by those who are asleep are very similar to things seen by those who are awake? But he who is certain about the knowledge of his own life does not say in it, "I know that I am awake," but "I know that I live"; whether he, therefore, sleeps, or whether he is awake, he lives. He cannot be deceived in his knowledge of this even by dreams. (XV.12.21)

Descartes offers two different responses to the epistemological dream problem. The first response resembles Augustine's; it is to say that certain claims to knowledge are immune to this threat (let us call this the "immunity response"). Thus Descartes comments in the *Passions of the Soul* that "even if we are asleep and dreaming, we cannot feel sad, or moved by any other passion, unless the soul truly has this passion within it" (I.26; AT XI, 349; CSM I, 338). It follows, I take it, that if I feel sad I *am* sad and can know this, whether or not I know I am dreaming. This reassurance recalls the above-quoted passage from Augustine's *Against the Academics*.

At the end of Meditation V, Descartes offers another version of the immunity response:

> Can one raise the objection I put to myself a while ago, that I may be dreaming, or that everything which I am now thinking has as little truth as what comes to the mind of one who is asleep? Yet even this does not change anything. For even though I might be dreaming, if there is anything which is evi-

dent to my intellect, then it is wholly true. (AT VII, 70–71; CSM
II, 49; cf. CSM II, 310)[1]

That version of the immunity response recalls several passages from Augustine's *Against the Academics,* including this
one:

> But it is manifest that no matter in what condition I am, if there
> [are] one and six worlds, there are in all seven worlds, and I
> unhesitatingly assert that I know this. Now, then, convince me
> that this combination or the abovementioned disjunctions can
> be not true by reason of sleep, madness, or the unreliability of
> the senses; and if being awakened from my slumber I recall
> them, I shall allow that I am vanquished. (III.11.25)

Here, in an intriguing passage from *The Immortality of the Soul,*
Augustine seems to be making a very general point along
much the same lines:

> If, for instance, someone during a dream has appeared to him-
> self to be engaged in a discussion and, pursuing true principles,
> has learned something in this discussion, then these true princi-
> ples also remain the same and unchangeable after his awaken-
> ing. Yet, other circumstances may be found untrue, such as the
> place of the discussion, or the person with whom he seemed to
> have the discussion, and—as far as their sound is concerned—
> even the words seemingly used in the discussion, and other
> things of such kind as are to be perceived, or acted upon,
> through the senses by awakened persons. Yet, these things pass
> away and in no way reach the level of everlasting presence of
> true principles. From this, one may conclude that, through a
> bodily change such as sleep, the soul's use of the same body can
> be reduced, but not the soul's proper life. (14.23)

1. Compare this passage from the *Principles* (I.30): "And as for our senses,
if we notice anything here that is clear and distinct, no matter whether we are
awake or asleep, then provided we separate it from what is confused and
obscure we will easily recognize—whatever the thing in question—which are
the aspects that may be regarded as true" (AT VIIIA, 17; CSM II, 203).

An especially interesting version of the immunity response is what we might call the "general illusion response." It is to say that what dreams are most likely to deceive us about, namely, the presence or the appearance of particular physical objects, is something our senses may deceive us about even when we are awake. The remedy for that sort of liability to error is the proper use of reason. Reason, according to this response, can deal with the illusions of our dreams no less effectively than with the illusions of our waking life. So again, even if we do not know whether we are now dreaming, there are lots of other things we can now know.

Here, in a passage from near the end of the *Discourse*, Part IV, Descartes moves in a particularly effective way from the immunity response to the general illusion response:

> But once the knowledge of God and the soul has made us certain of this rule [the rule that everything we conceive very clearly and very distinctly is true], it is easy to recognize that the things we imagine in dreams should in no way make us doubt the truth of the thoughts we have when awake. For if one happened even in sleep to have some very distinct idea (if, say, a geometer devised some new proof), one's being asleep would not prevent the idea from being true. And as to the most common error of our dreams, which consists in their representing various objects to us in the same way as our external senses do, it does not matter that this gives us occasion to doubt the truth of such ideas, for often they can also mislead us without our being asleep—as when those with jaundice see everything coloured yellow, or when stars or other very distant bodies appear to us much smaller than they are. For after all, whether we are awake or asleep, we ought never to let ourselves be convinced except by the evidence of our reason. (AT VI, 39; CSM I, 130–31)

The immunity response, though it is put forward without qualification by both Augustine and Descartes, is clearly rejected by other philosophers. Plato, in Book IX of the *Re-*

public, suggests that dreaming occurs when reason sleeps and the irrational part of the soul "casts off sleep, and seeks to find a way to its gratification" (571c). For Plato the dream state would therefore seem to be, by its very nature, irrational. Aquinas thinks of sleep as fettering reason (*Summa theologiae,* 2a.2ae.154.5). He distinguishes four grades of sleep, from the deepest, which he says is dreamless, to the lightest, in which, according to him, the sleeper's judgment is almost free. Yet, if we reason during even the lightest grade of sleep, Aquinas assures us, when we wake up we invariably recognize that we have made a mistake (1a.84.8.ad2).

Descartes's second response to the epistemological dream problem (let us call this one the "coherence response") is the best known, although it has been almost universally derided. It appears at the end of Meditation VI in this famous passage:

> Accordingly, I should not have any further fears about the falsity of what my senses tell me every day; on the contrary, the exaggerated doubts of the last few days should be dismissed as laughable. This applies especially to the principal reason for doubt, namely my inability to distinguish being asleep and being awake. For I now notice that there is a vast difference between the two, in that dreams are never linked by memory with all the other actions of life as waking experiences are. If, while I am awake, anyone were suddenly to appear to me and then disappear immediately, as happens in sleep, so that I could not see where he had come from or where he had gone to, it would not be unreasonable for me to judge that he was a ghost, or a vision created in my brain, rather than a real man. But when I distinctly see where things come from and where and when they come to me, and when I can connect my perceptions of them with the whole of the rest of my life without a break, then I am quite certain that when I encounter these things I am not asleep but awake. (AT VII, 89–90; CSM II, 61–62)

For rather obvious reasons, readers of Descartes have always been dissatisfied with the coherence response to the epistemological dream problem. For one thing, we may doubt that dreams are characteristically, let alone invariably, disjoint in themselves, or incoherent with the rest of our conscious experience. To speak from my own experience, dreams *are* sometimes "linked by memory with all the other actions of life as waking experiences are"—not often, to be sure, but occasionally.

Even if we were to assume with Descartes that dreams are invariably incoherent, both internally and externally, there is an even more serious difficulty. I can surely *dream* them to be otherwise; that is, it seems quite conceivable that I could dream that my dream experience satisfied Descartes's criterion for waking life. The epistemological dream problem would then persist in the question, How do I know that my experience really satisfies the tests for waking experience, as opposed to my being in a dream and only dreaming that my experience satisfies those tests?

Perhaps Hobbes was the first person to express this last dissatisfaction with Descartes. His expression is succinct and effective:

> Consider someone who dreams that he is in doubt as to whether he is dreaming or not. My question is whether such a man could not dream that his dream fits in with his ideas of a long series of past events. If this is possible, then what appear to the dreamer to be actions belonging to his past life could be judged to be true occurrences, just as if he were awake. (Objections III; AT VII, 195; CSM II, 137)

Descartes's reply to Hobbes is disappointing. He insists, first, that, whatever might seem to the dreamer to be the case at the time, "a dreamer cannot really connect his dreams with the ideas of past events" (AT VII, 196). One wants to know, first, how Descartes can be so sure of this, and, second, why, even if it is so, it rules out the dreamer's simply dreaming that the coherence test has been passed. Descartes adds that "when he wakes up, he will easily recognize his mistake." But, again, the reply sidesteps the problem.[2]

The coherence response is not found elsewhere in Descartes's writings. It is not immediately obvious why he offers it at all. If Descartes had supposed that one's knowledge claims were put in jeopardy by the mere passage of time and had therefore constantly to be rebuttressed by fresh reconstructions of the foundations of knowledge, then the epistemological dream problem would present an ever-renewable threat. In that case one might find some solace in even so desperate a reply as the coherence response. But Descartes states explicitly at the very beginning of Meditation I that it "was necessary, *once in the course of my life,* to demolish everything completely and start again right from the foundations" (AT VII, 17; CSM II, 12, emphasis added). The same idea appears at the beginning of the *Principles:* "It seems that the only way of freeing ourselves from these opinions is to make the effort, *once in the course of our life,* to doubt everything which we find to contain even the smallest suspicion of uncertainty" (AT VIII, 5; CSM I, 193, emphasis added).

Apparently, then, it is Descartes's idea that the rational reconstruction of knowledge is something that needs to be performed by us individually for ourselves; it is something that, once done by me, stays done for me, and similarly for anyone else who carries it out. In view of this, the coherence response seems not only ineffective but also uncalled for. Surely it would have been better to rest with some version of the immunity response. The immunity response is appropriate be-

<hr />

2. Robert Hanna has tried to convince me that there is another test suggested in this passage from the end of Meditation VI, namely, the test of "distinctly see[ing] where things come from and where and when they come to me." The idea is that this test of the distinct intuition of causes would have an epistemically guaranteeing character about it like that of clear and distinct perception generally. Hanna's suggestion is tantalizing, but I find no solid basis for it in Descartes's epistemology. If Descartes intended it as something distinct from the coherence test, which is certainly not obvious from the text, then he failed to provide the required epistemological *bona fides* for it.

cause, instead of having me try to show that I can know now whether I am now dreaming, it leaves me to maintain that the dream threat need not undermine crucial knowledge claims of other sorts.

Augustine has no such project as Descartes's rational reconstruction of knowledge. What he wants to do is answer global skepticism. But to answer global skepticism he needs only vindicate sample knowledge claims in the face of the most clever attacks the global skeptic can mount. When the epistemological dream problem is directed against such claims as "I know that I exist," "I know that something tastes sweet to me," and "I know that 6 + 1 = 7," the immunity response seems effective. Appropriately, it is the only response to be found in Augustine.

৯৯

I say the immunity response seems effective. But is either Augustine or Descartes entitled to this response?

Certainly Descartes thinks of himself as needing to establish entitlement. After all, near the end of Meditation I he had considered that he might "go wrong every time [he adds] two and three or count[s] the sides of a square" (AT VII, 21; CSM II, 14). How does he know that he does not (as Aquinas supposes one always does) go wrong in his dreams?

In Meditation III, Descartes makes it clear that only by appealing to the existence and nature of God can he show himself entitled to rely on his most privileged store of putative truths:

> But what about when I was considering something very simple and straightforward in arithmetic or geometry, for example that two and three added together make five, and so on? Did I not see at least these things clearly enough to affirm their truth? . . . whenever my preconceived belief in the supreme power of God comes to mind, I cannot but admit that it would be easy for

him, if he so desired, to bring it about that I go wrong even in those matters which I think I see utterly clearly with my mind's eye. . . . But in order to remove even this slight reason for doubt, as soon as the opportunity arises I must examine whether there is a God, and, if there is, whether he can be a deceiver. For if I do not know this, it seems that I can never be quite certain about anything else. (AT VII, 35–36; CSM II, 25)

At the end of Meditation V, after Descartes has offered his second argument for God's existence and nature, he fills out his immunity response with the rule of clarity and distinctness:

Now, however, I have perceived that God exists, and at the same time I have understood that everything else depends on him, and that he is no deceiver; and I have drawn the conclusion that everything which I clearly and distinctly perceive is of necessity true. . . . Can one raise the objection I put to myself a while ago, that I may be dreaming, or that everything which I am now thinking has as little truth as what comes to the mind of one who is asleep? Yet even this [that is, the possibility that I may be dreaming] does not change anything. For even though I might be dreaming, if there is anything which is evident to my intellect, then it is wholly true.

Thus I see plainly that the certainty and truth of all knowledge depends uniquely on my knowledge of the true God, to such an extent that I was incapable of perfect knowledge about anything else until I knew him. (AT VII, 70–71; CSM II, 48–49)

So it is "knowing God," as Descartes himself puts it, that entitles him to use the rule of clarity and distinctness. And thus it is knowing God that entitles him to use the immunity response to answer the epistemological dream problem.

Augustine is no less insistent than Descartes about being entitled to use the immunity response to the epistemological dream problem. But he has no principled or criterial way of identifying those truths he can know, even in a dream.[3] Nor does he have any argument from the existence or nature of God that could be used to back up a rule or criterion like that of clarity and distinctness. He simply insists, without further backing, that his knowledge of certain specified truths is immune to any doubt that might arise from recognizing the possibility that he might then be dreaming.

❧

The question, 'How do I know whether I* am now dreaming?' is one of the most interesting, as well as one of the most perplexing, 'I*' questions ever asked. Its prominence in the philosophies of Augustine and Descartes is both striking and important. The other 'I*' question about dreams that most interests Descartes I discuss in the next chapter. And the other one that most interests Augustine I shall take up in Chapter 8.

3. The significance of this lack should become clearer in Chapters 10 and 13.

[6]

The Metaphysical
Dream Problem

When Hobbes chides Descartes for his lack of origi-
nality in posing dream problems, he runs together the epistemological dream problem ('How do I know whether I* am
now dreaming?') with another problem, one I call the "metaphysical dream problem" ('How do I know that not all life is
my* dream?'). With respect to this second problem, Hobbes's
charge that Descartes only rehashes "ancient material" is certainly unfounded. This problem is not to be found in Plato,
or, I think, in the ancient skeptics. It is almost broached in this
remarkable passage from Augustine's *Against the Academics:*

> "But," he asks, "how do you know that the world you speak of
> exists at all? The senses may deceive." No matter how you ar-
> gued, you were never able to repudiate the value of the senses
> to the extent that you could convince us that nothing appears to
> us to be. . . . By the term 'world,' then, I mean this, whatever
> kind of thing it be, which surrounds and nourishes us and
> which presents itself to my eyes and seems to me to hold earth
> and sky or quasi-earth and quasi-sky. If you say that non-reality
> presents itself to me, I shall still be free from error. It is he who
> rashly judges what presents itself to him to be actual reality that
> falls into error. . . . But you will ask me: "If you are asleep, does
> the world which you now see exist?" I have already said that

whatever presents itself to me in that way, I call "world."
(III.11.24–25)

Here Augustine formulates the notion of an individual subject's phenomenal world. He does so in response to the skeptical taunt, "But what if you are dreaming?" There is a world of
my present conscious experience, Augustine replies; I can
know that it exists and has such and such a character, even if I
do not know whether it is a world whose existence is independent of me, or whether, instead, it is only my private and
ephemeral dream world. Explicitly, then, we have here only
the familiar immunity response to the epistemological dream
problem. But in this passage Augustine comes tantalizingly
close to doing something more. His proposal that one might
call the sum of one's impressions of "outside" things "the
world" suggests the metaphysical dream problem. Having established the existence of his phenomenal world and having
claimed direct knowledge of it and its character, he could
easily have gone on to ask whether, and, if so, how, he knows
there exists a world "beyond" this "dream world."

He could have, but he does not. The metaphysical dream
problem is not a problem Augustine ever explicitly raises.
Although he discusses sense perception in several places (e.g.,
Trinity, XI.2; *The Literal Meaning of Genesis*, XII) and certainly
discusses perceptual illusions, including the venerable oar in
water that appears bent (*The Literal Meaning of Genesis*,
XII.25.52), he never explicitly formulates the metaphysical
dream problem or makes any moves that seem clearly directed at solving that problem. As with his later use of cogito
reasoning, Augustine in the *Against the Academics* makes this
limited move merely to defeat global, or universal, skepticism.
I call what seems to be the object of my present experience
"the world," he says. I know that the world exists and that it
has such and such a character. Therefore, there is something
that I know. Global skepticism is defeated. A modern reader

naturally expects Augustine to go on to ask what lies behind one's phenomenal world, and how one knows—indeed, how one knows that there is anything at all beyond one's phenomenal world. But these expectations are never fulfilled. Notoriously, the expectation is fulfilled in Descartes. Indeed, it is Descartes who has inculcated this expectation in us. Here is a clear formulation from *The Search for Truth* of the progression of thought we have come to expect:

> But you cannot take it amiss if I ask whether you are not, like all men, liable to fall asleep, and whether you cannot think, while asleep, that you are seeing me, that you are walking in this garden, that the sun is shining—in brief, all the things of which you now believe you are utterly certain. Have you never heard this expression of astonishment in comedies: 'Am I awake or asleep?' How can you be certain that your life is not a continuous dream . . . ? (AT X, 511; CSM II, 407–8)

Breathlessly, and without any generalizing reflection or argumentative transition, Descartes moves directly in this passage from asking, "Am I awake or asleep, and how can I know?" to raising the further question, "How can I be certain that my life is not a continuous dream?" The question of how he knows that there is a real world of physical objects out there, beyond the phenomenal world and independent of its perception, is not answered in the *Meditations* until well into Meditation VI. By that time Descartes has proved, to his own satisfaction, anyway, that God exists and is a perfect being, that is, a being with all positive perfections. Descartes's "proof of the external world," as it has come to be called, relies on those claims, as well as on various scholastic distinctions between kinds of causality. The basic idea is that God would not, since he is no deceiver, give me the ideas I have of there being independent physical objects, unless there really were independent physical objects. "For," Descartes goes on,

God has given me no faculty at all for recognizing any such
source of these ideas [as something other than an independent
physical object]; on the contrary, he has given me a great pro-
pensity to believe that they are produced by corporeal things.
So I do not see how God could be understood to be anything
but a deceiver if the ideas were transmitted from a source other
than corporeal things. It follows that corporeal things exist. (AT
VII, 79–80; CSM II, 55)

How are the epistemological dream problem and the metaphysical dream problem related in Descartes? Some commentators have thought that there is to be found in Descartes a
line of reasoning that leads from the epistemological problem
directly to the metaphysical problem. One way this might be
true would be for Descartes to use the conclusion

(1)   I do not know whether I am now dreaming,

or perhaps

(2)   I never know whether I am then dreaming,

as a premise in an argument leading to the conclusion

(3)   For all I know, I am always dreaming.

Something like this seems to be W. H. Walsh's reading of
Descartes. Here Walsh identifies what he calls "the argument
from dreaming" right after having identified "the argument
from illusion":

> The argument from illusion begins with the assertion that there
> are occasions on which we are clearly mistaken in our percep-
> tual judgments and goes on to maintain that there is no intrinsic
> difference, at the time of their occurrence, between the percep-
> tual experiences we take to be veridical and those we subse-

quently reject as illusory; the conclusion is that we *may* be mistaken in *all* our perceptual judgments. The argument from dreaming proceeds on precisely the same lines, except that the initial premise is that we sometimes take objects to exist in reality when they exist only in our dreams and the conclusion that we may be dreaming all the time.[1]

Explicitly, the dream argument Walsh reconstructs from Descartes is this:

(4)   We sometimes take objects to exist in reality when they exist only in our dreams.

(5)   There is no intrinsic difference, at the time of their occurrence, between the perceptual experiences we take to be veridical and those we subsequently reject as illusory.

Therefore,

(6)   We may be dreaming all the time.

As it stands, the argument is formally invalid; it has the form '*p; q;* therefore *r*'. We are doubtless meant to fill it out to make it more plausible. Presumably we are meant to fill in a bridge principle along the following lines:

(7)   If [4] we sometimes take objects to exist in reality when they exist only in our dreams, and [5] there is no intrinsic difference, at the time of their occurrence, between the preceptual experiences we take to be veridical and those we subsequently reject as illusory, then [6] we may be dreaming all the time.

Walsh criticizes Descartes on the ground that, if (5) were correct, "we could never formulate the premise that we some-

1. W. H. Walsh, *Metaphysics* (London: Hutchinson University Library, 1963), 91.

times think we are perceiving things when all the time we are dreaming." He adds: "It would not be possible to say, as Descartes wants to say, things like 'I thought I was awake and sitting in my room, but it subsequently turned out that I was dreaming'."[2] Harry Frankfurt summarizes Walsh's criticism of Descartes this way:

> According to Walsh, then, the conclusion of the dream argument entails that it is impossible to distinguish between deceptive and non-deceptive experience. But the premisses of the argument, as he understands them, involve the use of this distinction. This is why he claims that if the conclusion of the argument is true its premisses cannot meaningfully be asserted, and that the argument exhibits "a fundamental incoherence."[3]

Frankfurt goes on to criticize Walsh on two counts. First, he says that Walsh's objection does not at all discredit the argument, if, as seems plausible, it is to be taken as a *reductio*. Moreover, a *reductio*, according to Frankfurt, would be "uniquely suited" to Descartes's purposes here. I agree with Frankfurt on this point. Second, Frankfurt insists that nothing "in the text of the *Meditations* supports Walsh's formulation of the conclusion of the dream argument."[4] Presumably Walsh takes (6) to be another way of putting Descartes's supposition near the end of Meditation I: "I shall think that the sky, the air, the earth, colours, shapes, sounds and all external things are merely the delusions of dreams which [the malicious demon] has devised to ensnare my judgement" (AT VII, 22; CSM II, 15). In a similar way, I have taken (3) to express this idea. But Frankfurt's point, and here too I agree with him, is that Descartes does not get to (6), or to (3), by gener-

2. Ibid.
3. Harry Frankfurt, *Demons, Dreamers, and Madmen* (Indianapolis: Bobbs-Merrill, 1970), 50.
4. Ibid.

alizing from (4), or from (2). The supposition of, first, a deceiving God, and then, a malicious demon, is an additional step in Descartes's reasoning.

Margaret Wilson offers an interpretation of Descartes that, she says, is more like Walsh's than Frankfurt's. She finds this argument in Descartes:

(8)   If I see no certain marks to distinguish waking experience of physical objects from dream experience when, I believe, I was deceived, then I have reason to believe my waking experience too may be deceptive.

(9)   I see no such marks.

Therefore,

(10)   I have reason to suppose that waking experience too may be deceptive (thoroughly delusory).

(11)   If I have reason to suppose but my waking experience may be deceptive (thoroughly delusory), then I have reason to doubt the existence of physical objects.

Therefore,

(12)   I have reason to doubt the existence of physical objects.

Wilson comments: "Here the source of doubt is not located in the problem of knowing one is awake; it is rather expressed in the claim that I cannot say *why I should unquestioningly regard waking experience of physical objects as real or veridical, when there are no marks to distinguish it from the 'illusions of dreams.'*"[5]

Wilson claims to find in Meditation I "a minor point of indirect support" for her interpretation. But we seem to need more than that to follow her reading. As I have already em-

---

5. Margaret Dauler Wilson, *Descartes* (London: Routledge & Kegan Paul, 1978), 23.

phasized, Descartes's reasoning in Meditation I to something like (3) makes use of, first, the suggestion that, for all I know, God might be deceiving me about the existence of the material world. Then, after that suggestion is put aside on the grounds that such deception would be incompatible with God's nature, Descartes suggests that there might be an evil genius deceiving me about this. As I see it, then, the core of Descartes's reasoning in this part of Meditation I is this:

(13) For all I know, some very powerful evil genius "has employed his whole energies in deceiving me."
(14) If (13) then, for all I know, "there is no earth, no heaven."

Thus,

(15) For all I know, "there is no earth."

The conclusion, (15), I have been expressing this way:

(15′) For all I know, all life is my dream.[6]

---

6. In an important respect, (15′) is a misleading way of expressing (15), as Bernard Williams brings out in these comments: "'How many times has it happened to me,' Descartes says in the *First Meditation* . . . 'that I dreamed that I was in this place, that I was dressed, that I was near the fire, when all the time I was in bed with no clothes on.' But this claim rests on counting some previous experiences as veridical: those of waking up, and so forth. It relies also on some inferences from those experiences to other physical facts, as that before waking up he was lying in bed. If the hyperbolical doubt were correct, there would be no such facts, and the experiences supposedly of waking up and so forth would themselves not have been veridical. It follows that the hyperbolical doubt is at least unhappily expressed by the thought that perhaps we dream all the time (as Descartes uncharacteristically puts it in the *Recherche de la vérité* [AT X, 511]); more importantly it follows that the hyperbolical doubt cannot in any way be supported by considerations drawn from taking these experiences as veridical, nor can it rest in any way on his knowing that he has, in the past, dreamed"; *Descartes,* 57–58. As Frankfurt points out, the reasoning could still be that of a *reductio.* It could be, but it is not.

Not only do (13–15) seem to capture the core of Descartes's reasoning in this passage, there seems to be no place, in Meditation I anyway, for Wilson's argument, (8–12). But let us take a closer look.

How is the consequent of (8) ("I have reason to believe that my waking life too may be deceptive") to be understood? Is the idea that (i) my waking life may *sometimes* be deceptive? or rather that (ii) my waking life may *always* be deceptive? Reading the consequent of (8) as (i) gives us something rather weak—hardly enough to make the conditional, (11), plausible. By adding in parentheses "thoroughly deceptive," Wilson seems to suggest the second reading. In any case, that is what we need to make (11) plausible. But that, in turn, makes (8) implausible. Why should "seeing no certain marks to distinguish waking experience of physical objects from dream experience when, I believe, I was deceived" give me reason to believe that my waking experience may *always* be deceptive?

It seems, then, that this argument would not have been a strong one for Descartes to use. Moreover, even if it does turn up, as Wilson urges, later on in the *Meditations,* it does not seem to be reasoning that one finds in Meditation I.

My assessment of the epistemological dream argument in Meditation I, and its connection to the metaphysical dream argument, fits well, I think, with that of Bernard Williams. Williams understands the epistemological argument to be part of a loosening-up strategy to free us from our prejudices so that we can entertain hyperbolical doubt and be ready for the metaphysical dream argument. As he puts the point, Descartes "progresses from the universal possibility of illusion to the possibility of universal illusion, but he does not try to infer the second from the first."[7]

ॐ

In posing the metaphysical dream problem, Descartes moves the first-personalization of philosophy significantly be-

7. Ibid., 54.

yond anything to be found in Augustine. There is a point in the rational reconstruction of knowledge, according to Descartes, at which I need to ask myself whether I know, and if so, how I know, that there even exists an external world for me to have knowledge of. No such question arises in Augustine. Even if solipsism is, within the course of the rational reconstruction of knowledge, only a rejected hypothesis, the fact that it is a hypothesis at all, and beyond that a hypothesis that needs to be rejected by argumentation, is a radical development.

M. F. Burnyeat argues that no ancient or medieval skeptic divides things up so that one's own body counts as part of something we have come to call "the external world."[8] It is Descartes, according to Burnyeat, who first does that. It is he who first presents solipsism as a position to be considered (and rejected). I agree with that assessment. But I should like to add that Augustine's failure to consider the possibility of solipsism is closely related to his failure to identify himself with his thought's ego.

In Chapter 4 we noted that Augustine asks, "What can the mind be certain that it* is?" but not, "What can I be certain that I* am?" By reasoning essentially routed through the 'it*' question, Augustine argues that the mind is an incorporeal, thinking thing. But he never considers the possibility that quite analogous reasoning could lead him, as it later leads Descartes, to the conclusion that *he** is an incorporeal, thinking thing. In failing to pose the metaphysical dream problem, Augustine fails to appreciate fully how philosophically problematic the relationship between himself and the corporeal world might be taken to be. It is not that he explicitly rejects solipsism (Descartes does that). It is rather that he, like all philosophers before Descartes, fails to consider solipsism as a philosophical possibility.

8. "Idealism and Greek Philosophy."

[7]

Present-Moment
Dream Skepticism

Here is a summary of the dream situation so far surveyed:

A. Both Augustine and Descartes present the epistemological dream problem; but only Descartes presents the metaphysical dream problem.

B. Augustine's sole response to the epistemological dream problem is the immunity response (Whether or not I am now dreaming, there are various things I can know for certain); Descartes also offers this response.

C. In addition to the immunity response, Descartes also offers the the coherence response to the epistemological dream problem (I can distinguish dreams from waking life by applying the criterion of coherence).

D. Unlike the immunity response, the coherence response seems to offer a way to know whether I am now dreaming; in Descartes this response appears at the end of Meditation VI and nowhere else. It has met with justified derision.

E. Descartes's solution to the metaphysical dream problem (i.e., his proof of the external world in Meditation VI) does not provide a solution to the epistemological dream problem; what this fact suggests is that I can know that not all life is my dream without having to know whether I am now dreaming.

To gain some modern perspective on these matters, it might be well to note that at least one twentieth-century philosopher's solution to the metaphysical dream problem, like Descartes's, leaves the epistemological dream problem unsolved. Here is Bertrand Russell's solution:

> There is no logical impossibility in the supposition that the whole of life is a dream, in which we ourselves create all the objects that come before us. But although this is not logically impossible, there is no reason whatever to suppose that it is true; and it is, in fact, a less simple hypothesis, viewed as a means of accounting for the facts of our own life, than the common-sense hypothesis that there really are objects independent of us, whose action on us causes our sensations.[1]

Appealing to a principle of simplicity, I have sufficient warrant for concluding, according to Russell, that not all life is my dream. But the principle of simplicity will not help me to know whether I am now dreaming.

Here, then, seems to be a good possibility. I can know that not all life is a dream I* am having even though there is no occasion on which I know for certain that I* am not then dreaming. Let us call this position "present-moment dream skepticism." In this chapter, I consider whether present-moment dream skepticism is a coherent position.

Present-moment dream skepticism consists in accepting these two claims:

(1)   For any given time t, I never know at t whether I* am dreaming at t.

(2)   I know that not all life is my* dream.

Present-moment dream skepticism fits remarkably well with Descartes. For one thing—this point seems to be lost in

1. *Problems of Philosophy* (New York: Oxford University Press, 1959), 22–23.

the secondary literature—Descartes does not explicitly raise, let alone solve, the epistemological dream problem, either in the *Discourse* or in the *Principles*. Here is the complete dream passage in Discourse IV: "[C]onsidering that the very thoughts we have while awake may also occur while we sleep without any of them being at that time true, I resolved to pretend that all the things that had ever entered my mind were no more true than the illusions of my dreams" (AT VI, 32; CSM I, 127). Clearly, the epistemological dream problem does not arise there. And here is the complete dream argument in the *Principles:* "[I]n our sleep we regularly seem to have sensory perception of, or to imagine, countless things which do not exist anywhere; and if our doubts are on the scale just outlined, there seem to be no marks by means of which we can with certainty distinguish being asleep from being awake" (AT VIIIA, 6; CSM I, 194).

Having first read the *Meditations,* we might expect this passage in the *Principles* to lead right into something about how I cannot know whether I* am now dreaming. But the paragraph ends there. And the first sentence of the paragraph makes it clear that the sentence I have quoted is meant to give one of two reasons for doubting "about the existence of the objects of sense-perception and imagination." Quite clearly this is the problem of the external world, that is, the metaphysical dream problem, and not the epistemological dream problem.

With respect to the *Meditations,* the situation is this. The famous dream passage in Meditation I includes the admission, "I see plainly that there are never any sure signs by means of which being awake can be distinguished from being asleep," and ends, "The result is that I begin to feel dazed, and this very feeling only reinforces the notion that I may be asleep" (AT VII, 19; CSM II, 13). The idea is clearly that I may *now* be asleep, that I do not know whether I* am *now* dreaming. I am left to generalize and conclude that I never know whether I* am *then* dreaming.

Descartes then brings in quite distinct considerations to show that I do not know whether all life is my* dream. There is, first, the tentative suggestion that an omnipotent God might have brought it about that "there is no earth, no sky, no extended thing, no shape, no size, no place, while at the same time ensuring that all these things appear to me to exist just as they do now" (AT VII, 21; CSM II, 14). Later the postulated malicious demon takes over for the omnipotent God and leads Descartes to embrace this possibility: "I shall think that the sky, the air, the earth, colours, shapes, sounds and all external things are merely the delusions of dreams which he has devised to ensnare my judgement" (AT VII, 22; CSM II, 15). In a recapitulatory section in Meditation VI, Descartes suggests that he has had this reason for doubting the existence of the external world: ". . . every sensory experience I have ever thought I was having while awake I can also think of myself as sometimes having while asleep; and since I do not believe that what I seem to perceive in sleep comes from things located outside me, I did not see why I should be any more inclined to believe this of what I think I perceive while awake" (AT VII, 77; CSM II, 53).

In his proof of the external world in Meditation VI, Descartes brings in considerations having to do with God's existence and nature to conclude that his ideas are transmitted from corporeal things as their source, and so he is not always dreaming. In this way he solves the metaphysical dream problem to his own satisfaction. As I have already remarked, it is not clear why Descartes then goes back to reconsider the epistemological dream problem, since he has already provided the immunity response to it and solved the metaphysical dream problem to his own satisfaction. But that is what he does. His coherence response comes at the very end of the *Meditations*. This response seems pretty obviously unsatisfactory—as many commentators have gleefully pointed out. Moreover, it does not seem to be doing any significant work in Descartes's rational reconstruction of knowledge—at least if that reconstruction is taken to be completed in the *Meditations*.

What I mean when I say that the coherence response does not seem to be doing any significant work is this. The epistemological dream problem might be thought to threaten Descartes's proof of the external world on the grounds that, if I never know that I* am not then dreaming, then, for all I ever know, the reasoning I use to prove the existence of the external world may be faulty. But the immunity response disarms that threat. My reasoning can be faultless, I can even now know that it is faultless, even though I do not know whether I* am now dreaming. So I can prove, it seems—without solving the epistemological dream problem—the existence and general nature of the external world (see the Appendix).

What remains under the threat of the epistemological dream problem? Presumably what remain are particular, contingent truths about the world, such as that I am sitting here at my computer, writing these words. But such truths do not figure in a Cartesian rational reconstruction of knowledge in his *Meditations*. The thought suggests itself that, perhaps, the epistemological dream problem is, for Descartes, a throwaway problem taken from a long tradition going back through Augustine to Plato, one that plays no significant role in his own thought.

≈⬤

Augustine seems to have set such high standards for knowledge that one could not have the knowledge that, for example, one is sitting by the fire anyway. In *Against the Academics* he suggests that what can be known is limited to what appears to one to be true in such a way that it could not appear that way and be false (III.9.21).[2] I take it to be a consequence of this restriction that I can gain knowledge through my senses

2. See Cicero, *Academica*, II.11.34.

only when something appears to me in such a way that I cannot be mistaken about it. But besides the dreaming possibility there are all sorts of other ways I might be wrong in thinking that I am sitting by the fire. The sensory presentations that pass Augustine's incorrigibility test (e.g., my tasting a sweet taste) are precisely those that, Augustine tells us, are also safe from the threat that I might now be dreaming.

Augustine does allow that there is a loose or improper sense of 'know' (*scire*) in which we can be said to know much more than the proper sense allows:

> It is true that when we speak properly, we are said to know only what we apprehend with the mind's firm reason. But when we speak in language which is better suited to common use—as even Holy Scripture speaks—we should not hesitate to say we know both what we have perceived by our bodily senses and what we believe of trustworthy witnesses, while understanding the distance between the latter and the former. (*Retractions* I.13.3)

Presumably in the loose sense of 'know' I could be said to know both that I* am sitting by the fire and that I* am not now dreaming, even though, in the proper and philosophical sense, I know neither one.

Does Augustine think that, in the strict and proper sense of 'know', I can know that not all life is my* dream? It seems so, but it is also odd to claim that he does, since he never raises the question. There are passages in Augustine that could be taken as suggesting that one sometimes recognizes that one* is then awake. Consider this one from the *Confessions,* in which he is discussing neither the epistemological nor the metaphysical dream problem but the moral dream problem:

> Yet the difference between waking and sleeping is so great that even when, during sleep, it happens otherwise [i.e., I do not remember my chaste resolutions or abide by them but instead indulge my sexual appetite] I return to a clear conscience when

I wake and realize that, because of this difference, I was not responsible for the act, although I am sorry that by some means or other it happened in me. (X.30)

Augustine's talk about a great difference between dreams and waking life, and his bravado about a clear conscience once he has recognized that what had just gone on was only a dream, suggests that when I awake from a dream I know, not only that not all life is my dream, but even that I am now awake. Yet he never meets the skeptical challenge, "What if you are only dreaming?" with the reply, "I just awoke from a dream and I can recognize incorrigibly that this is the real thing—waking life in living color!" I am inclined to suppose that he thinks he can never know that he* is then awake, even though he does know that he* is sometimes awake; that is, I am inclined to suppose that he accepts present-moment dream skepticism.

To bring out what I surmise Augustine's position to be, let me suggest an analogy. My clock radio has illuminated numbers that display the time of day. The clock has two settings that control the brightness of those numerals. If I just look at the display, without flipping the switch to change the brightness, I am usually unsure whether the numerals are bright or dull. I need to flip the switch to determine, by contrast, what the original setting was. Augustine seems to suppose that waking up from a dream is like flipping a switch that reveals the previous illumination to have been dull.

There is, however, a complication. It may be only in a dream that I am waking up. The wake-up experience in the dream may be bright by comparison with what went before it (*in the dream*) and yet be dull by comparison with an experience yet to come. In fact, for any given bright-dull contrast I "observe," I may not be able to tell at the time whether it will be upstaged by an even brighter experience.

Still—and here I am making up an Augustinian argument, not reconstructing any text known to me—given that some of our experiences are "brighter" than others, there is, for each of us, a de facto supreme brightness to our experiences; that is, for each of us there is a brightness to some of our experiences that is never, in fact, outshone by any yet brighter experience. Experience that has that brightness is, for each of us, just what waking life is. I can know that I* have experience that is, in fact, never outshone by any yet brighter experience without ever knowing, in the proper and philosophical sense, that I* am then having it. And hence I can know that not all life is my* dream, even though I never know whether I* am then dreaming.

One may want to protest that this last response, on behalf of Augustine, does not meet the skeptical challenge. We can be justified in supposing that there is a de facto brightness about some of our experiences without being justified in supposing that those supremely bright experiences are all experiences of the external world. The maddening point of the metaphysical dream problem seems to be the frustrating truth that no quality at all of our experiences themselves is a guarantee that they are experiences of the external world rather than just dream experiences.

Suppose there is some quality Q (brightness, clear definition, whatever) which certain of our experiences have, such that every experience with Q is in fact an experience of the external world. Since Q is by hypothesis a quality of the experience itself, it seems Q could be replicated in a dream experience. To know that it never is, we would need some way of getting outside our waking and dream experiences to see that, every time Q belongs to the experience, the external world is there as pictured. But there is no way of getting outside our experiences to make such a correlation.

In responding to this challenge we need to remind ourselves that it goes well beyond anything Augustine ever considers. For Augustine there is no notion of the external world, to which all bodies, including my own, belong. As we saw in the previous chapter, Descartes, with his metaphysical dream problem, develops such a notion; but the metaphysical dream problem is not to be found in Augustine. For him, the position I am calling present-moment dream skepticism certainly includes the claim, "I know that I am sometimes awake," but it does not include 'I know that I sometimes have experiences that are correlated with the external world in such a way as to be experiences of such a world."

The brightness test might or might not be the best way we have of dividing our experiences into dream experiences and waking ones. But it seems to be at least a good candidate for trying to make sense of the claims, suggested by Augustine's various remarks, that (i) I can *know* that there are times when I am awake, (ii) I sometimes *seem* to be able to tell that I am then awake, but, in fact, (iii) I never really know, at the time, that I am then awake. (The reason I never really know at the time is that I cannot then know whether the brightness of that experience will be outdone by an even brighter brightness.)

෪

Quite apart from what Descartes or Augustine thought, or might be imagined to have thought, can we say for ourselves that present-moment dream skepticism is a stable position? Many philosophers, beginning with Hobbes, have assumed that present-moment dream skepticism is in fact an *unstable,* or even incoherent, position; that is, many philosophers have assumed that reflection on

(1)   For any given time t, I never know at t whether I* am dreaming at t

leads ineluctably to the conclusion

(2′)   I do not know whether all life is my* dream.

A simple way to argue for this conclusion is to appeal to the conditional 'If (1), then (2′)' or, perhaps, to this variant:

(3)   If there is never a time at which I know that I* am
      not then dreaming, then, for all I know, I* am always
      dreaming.

Statement (3) has some immediate appeal. But is it really satisfactory? In particular, does the plausibility of (3) rest on anything more substantial than an illicit quantifier shift? It may
lose some of its appeal when we consider analogies such as
this:

(4)   If there is never a time at which I know that I am not
      going to breathe another breath, then, for all I know,
      I am always going to breathe another breath.

I reject (4) because I can know that I am mortal and hence will
sometime breathe a last breath, without having to recognize
any specific breath as my last.
     Or suppose that I have been given the task of counting
marbles in large bags of marbles. Then consider this claim:

(5)   If there is never a time at which I know that I have
      just counted marbles without making a mistake, then,
      for all I know, I always make mistakes in counting
      marbles.

Suppose, now, that I keep counting the marbles in a given bag
and, except for one time, always get the the same answer, say,
'137.' Suppose that I get this answer 98 times out of 99. Now
suppose that I recount the bag and get, for the 99th time out
of 100, the result '137.' There is still the possibility that I have
made canceling mistakes this time (e.g., repeating '14' and
skipping '56'). But by getting the same result so many times I
have ample justification, ceteris paribus, for the knowledge
claim that I do not always make a mistake in counting marbles.
     Might one want to say something similar about (3)? I think
so. There could certainly be general reasons for saying that

not all life is my dream that would leave me without a means of coming to know on specific occasions whether I am then dreaming. Descartes's proof of the external world offers one such reason. Russell's argument from simplicity suggests another. And here is a much simpler, not to say simplistic, argument for the same conclusion:

(6)   Normally healthy people are sometimes awake.
(7)   I am a normally healthy person.

Therefore,

(8)   I am sometimes awake.

Barry Stroud seems to want to rule out what I am calling present-moment dream skepticism, but he has a different principle in mind from (3): "[Descartes] realizes that if everything he can ever learn about what is happening in the world around him comes to him through the senses, but he cannot tell by means of the senses whether or not he is dreaming, then all the sensory experiences he is having are compatible with his merely dreaming of a world around him. . . ."[3] This passage suggests the following conditional:

(9)   If (a) everything Descartes can ever learn about what is happening in the world around him comes through the senses, and (b) on no occasion can Descartes tell by means of the senses whether he is then dreaming, then (c) it is compatible with all Descartes can learn from his senses that he is always dreaming.

In fact, the surrounding discussion in Stroud's book suggests a conditional that is stronger than (9) in two respects. For one

3. *The Significance of Philosophical Scepticism* (New York: Oxford University Press, 1984), 12.

thing, it becomes clear that Stroud does not want to limit Descartes's skepticism merely to putative knowledge about "what is happening in the world about him," that is, to what is *going on* in the world (as contrasted, say, with its structure or nature). "What we gain through the senses is on Descartes's view," Stroud writes in the next paragraph, "only information that is compatible with our dreaming things about the world around us and not knowing *anything* about that world."[4] So (9a) should be strengthened to, 'If (a) everything Descartes can ever learn about the world around him comes through the senses'. But then (9c) can be strengthened as well. For if everything Descartes can ever learn about the world around him comes through the senses and on no occasion can he tell by means of those senses whether he is then dreaming, then it is simply *compatible with all he can know* that he is always dreaming. So the Stroudian suggestion is now something like this:

(9′)   If (a) everything Descartes can ever learn about the world around him comes through the senses, and (b) on no occasion can Descartes tell by means of the senses whether he is then dreaming, then (c) it is compatible with all Descartes ever knows that he is always dreaming.

A first thing to note about (9′) is that clause (a) adds a restriction we have not considered so far. Stroud asks in effect whether, *given that all Descartes can ever learn about the world around him comes through his senses,* (1) for him leads ineluctably to the rejection of (2). In fact, Descartes's actual proof of the external world in Meditation VI rejects clause (a). It is from the existence and nature of God that Descartes thinks he can learn that there exists an external world that corresponds in certain important ways to his ideas. Stroud, of course, realizes

4. Ibid., 12, emphasis added.

this. He restricts himself explicitly to the reasoning in Meditation I.[5]

Let us continue briefly with the Stroudian reconstruction of Meditation I. Is present-moment dream skepticism an unstable position if one supposes that all one can ever learn about the world comes through the senses? Stroud's defense of (9′) is simple. He first argues that, for example,

(10) I know that I am sitting by the fire

is incompatible with, that is, entails the falsity of

(11) I am now dreaming.

Furthermore, not only is (11) incompatible with (10), I know it is incompatible. But

(12) If A knows that p, then A knows the falsity of everything A knows to be incompatible with his knowing that p.[6]

Thus, since

(13) I know that (10) is incompatible with (11),

therefore,

(14) I know that I am not now dreaming.

But since, according to Stroud, Descartes is right about there being no certain marks to distinguish dreams from waking life, (14) is guaranteed to be false. Therefore (10) is also false.

5. Ibid., 13.
6. Ibid., 29.

By a *reductio* argument I may conclude that I *do not* know that I am sitting by the fire.

Since (12) is perfectly general, all sorts of knowledge claims relevantly like (10) can be shown, using (12), to yield (14). And so, using *reductio* arguments like the one just rehearsed, I can show, it seems, that they are all false.

Let me pause at this point long enough to remark that, although (12) has a great deal of intuitive plausibility, there are many considerations besides the epistemological dream problem—roughly, other illusion possibilities, including even the possibility that I might be a brain in a vat—that might bring us to reject it. A proper treatment of those other considerations would, however, require a lengthy discussion. So, for purposes of this context, I simply accept (12) and move on.

The concluding step in Stroud's argument consists in surmising that all the knowledge I might suppose myself to have about the external world either can be put into claims like (10) or else rests ultimately on claims like (10) that entail the falsity of (11). But is that really so? Consider these claims:

(15) I know that normally healthy people are sometimes awake.

(16) I know that I am a normally healthy person.

It is not at all obvious that (15) or (16) entails the falsity of

(11) I am now dreaming.

At least, the sort of reasoning Stroud uses to support the idea that

(10) I know that I am sitting by the fire

entails (14) does not do the job here. That reasoning relies on the idea that I need to be having a certain sort of sensory input to know that I am now sitting by the fire; thus it is not enough to be sitting, asleep, by the fire and dreaming that that is what I am doing. But surely I do not need to be having any particular sort of sensory input to know that normally healthy people are sometimes awake, or that I am a normally healthy person. What would that required sort of sensory input be?

Someone might suppose that no statement like (15) or (16) is true unless a host of experiential knowledge claims like these are true:

(17) I know that I am now reading a book about the sleep habits of normally healthy people.

(18) I know that I am now being examined by a doctor.

That supposition could, in fact, be taken to be part of the import of the Stroudian restriction: if one supposes that all one can ever learn about the world comes through the senses. But (15) does not entail (17) in particular. Nor does (16) entail (18). Does (15) at least entail that *some* specific, experiential, first-person, present-moment knowledge claim or other, which would give part of my evidence for (15), is true? And does (16) similarly entail that some such claim, which would give part of my evidence for (16), is true? Not, I think, except on the assumption of a strongly foundationalist analysis of sensory knowledge. The needed analysis would require that any true nonexperiential knowledge claim I make about the empirical world.be backed up by appropriate experiential knowledge I can truly claim to have. I do not rule out the possibility that some acceptable, strong version of foundationalism may some day be put forward. But we are hardly in a position now to disallow other accounts of sensory knowledge, even nonfoundationalist ones. So we cannot say that (15) and (16) could not be true unless various claims relevantly like (17) and (18) were also true. And so my not knowing whether I am now dreaming does not show us, by Stroud's reasoning, that (15) and (16) are false.

Someone might protest that moving away from the assumption of a strongly foundationalist account of sensory knowledge cuts this problem off from its Cartesian moorings. But that protest would be misplaced. As I have already indicated, Descartes does not accept Stroud's clause about supposing that all one can ever learn of the world comes through the senses. Had we wanted to keep our discussion Cartesianly pure, we would have had to reject that clause out of hand. It would then have been even easier to defend the stability of present-moment dream skepticism.

As far as we have been able to determine, then, present-moment dream skepticism is a philosophically stable position. Although Augustine seems never to ask himself whether all life is a dream he* is having, he proceeds as if he knew it were not. Present-moment dream skepticism is his implicit position. If we imagine Descartes lopping off the last seven sentences of the *Meditations* (a loss that might have been, for him, a significant gain), then present-moment dream skepticism would, perhaps, be Descartes's position, too. I myself find it alternately appealing and appalling. In any case, it deserves serious consideration as a response to these two dream problems.

What implications does, or should, present-moment dream skepticism have for the way we lead our lives? In particular, should the conviction that, for all I ever know at any given moment, I might at that moment be dreaming lead me to take my waking life less seriously? Or should it lead me to take my dream life more seriously? Or should I both take my dream life more seriously and my waking life less seriously? Augustine was led, I think, to take his dream life more seriously. But that is the subject of the next chapter.

[8]

The Moral Dream Problem

Plato is our earliest source, not only for the epistemological dream problem, but also for what I call "the moral dream problem" ('Am I morally responsible for what I* do or think in my dreams?'). With his natural flair for drama, Plato presents his version of this problem in terms of a natural symmetry. What we normally call sleep, he suggests, is only the sleep of reason. Our dreams occur when our appetites wake within us and, unbridled by reason, go on a rampage.

> Some of our unnecessary pleasures and desires seem to me lawless. . . .
> What desires do you mean?
> Those that are aroused during sleep . . . whenever the rest of the soul, the reasonable, gentle, and ruling part, is slumbering; whereas the wild and animal part, full of food and drink, skips about, casts off sleep, and seeks to find a way to its gratification. You know that there is nothing it will not dare to do at that time, free of any control by shame or prudence. It does not hesitate, as it thinks, to attempt sexual intercourse with a mother or anyone else—man, god, or beast; it will commit any foul murder and does not refrain from any kind of food. In a word, it will not fall short of any folly or shameless deed. (*Republic*, IX, 571bd)

Plato does not have his character Socrates worry in this passage about whether, when his dream self commits, say, incest with his mother, he is directly or only indirectly shamed. Perhaps committing incest in a dream is like doing something terrible in a drugged or drunken state. Or perhaps it is more like having your watchdogs break loose from their pens and maul your neighbor's sheep, all because you have not properly chained them up. Is dreaming that you are doing something *actually doing* something, even if only in a state of diminished responsibility, and even if what you do fails to have the consequences doing it in waking life would have? Or is doing something in a dream having something *happen to* you, perhaps something you are wholly or partly responsible for, but not because you, yourself, did it? Though these questions are not asked in this passage, they seem to be answered, at least implicitly. Here is the advice Plato gives us through his character Socrates:

> On the other hand, when a healthy and moderate man who has come to understand himself goes to sleep after rousing his reasonable part and feasting it on fine discussions and speculations but neither starving nor surfeiting his appetites, these appetites will slumber, and neither their pleasure nor their pain will disturb his best part, but they will allow it, pure and by itself, to look for and reach toward the perception of what he does not know, be it past, present, or future; if he has further, in the same manner, soothed his spirited part and has not gone to sleep with ruffled feelings after an outburst of anger, then having quieted both spirit and appetites, he arouses his third part in which intelligence resides and thus takes his rest; you know that it is then that he best grasps reality, and the visions which appear in his dreams are the least lawless. (571d–572b)

Plato's advice suggests that I am responsible for the actions of my dream self, not because what my dream self does is something that, strictly speaking, I do, but because my irrational impulses get expressed through the actions of my dream self and because those impulses are actually part of me and are potentially, through foresight, under my control. A bad dream is, in a way, something that happens to me, rather than something I do; but I can bring it about that bad dreams do not happen to me—that I do not have them. Their occurrence is, therefore, indirectly, even if not directly, my fault.

As we see below, Augustine would also like to offer this response to the moral dream problem; but it seems that such a way out of blame is not open to him. He is deeply concerned about the moral dream problem, but the immunity response he offers to the epistemological dream problem puts severe restrictions on his options for dealing with it. The moral dream problem finds expression in various of Augustine's writings; it is presented most emphatically, perhaps, in this passage from Book X of the *Confessions:*

> You commanded me not to commit fornication. . . . You gave me the grace and I did your bidding. . . . But in my memory . . . the images of things imprinted upon it by my former habits still linger on. When I am awake they obtrude themselves upon me, though with little strength. But when I dream, they not only give me pleasure but are very much like acquiescence in the act. The power which these illusory images have over my soul and my body is so great that what is no more than a vision can influence me in sleep in a way that the reality cannot do when I am awake. Surely it cannot be that when I am asleep I am not myself, O Lord my God? And yet the moment when I pass from wakefulness to sleep, or return again from sleep to wakefulness, marks a great difference in me. During sleep where is my reason which, when I am awake, resists such suggestions and remains firm and undismayed even in face of the realities themselves? Is it sealed off when I close my eyes? Does it fall asleep with the senses of the body? And why is it that even in sleep I often resist the attractions of these images, for I remember my chaste resolutions and abide by them and give no consent to temptations of this sort? Yet the difference between waking and

sleeping is so great that even when, during sleep, it happens otherwise, I return to a clear conscience when I awake and realize that, because of this difference, I was not responsible for the act, although I am sorry that by some means or other it happened in me. [*Nos non fecisse, quod tamen in nobis quoquo modo factum esse doleamus*—we have not done what we nevertheless regret has in some way or other been done in us.] (*Confessions*, X.30)

When Augustine says that the images of his dreams are "very much like acquiescence in the act" he may mean only that the experience of having sex in one's dream is very much like the experience of having sex in waking life. There is evidence, however, that he was worried about the behavior of his genital organs during sleep and, in particular, about having wet dreams; in *The Literal Meaning of Genesis* (XII.15.31) he refers to times when "in our sleep there appear images which naturally move the flesh" so that "what nature has gathered together it discharges through the organs of generation."

A philosopher can easily be impressed with the isolation, even with the inaccessibility, of one's own dream world. Both the epistemological dream problem and the metaphysical dream problem threaten significant ego isolation. Augustine, however, seems impressed by something quite different—by the defenseless exposure of a dreamer to observation by others. In particular, he seems worried that a genital erection and emission might be public evidence of an unchaste dream episode.

Most of us do not suppose that we are responsible for what we do in our dreams. But why not? More particularly, is there a good reason to deny that one is responsible for the acts of one's dream self? Here are three candidates:

(1)   My dream self is not really me; for this reason, if for no other, I am not directly responsible for what my

dream self does or thinks, even if I am somehow indirectly responsible.

(2)   What I do or think in my dreams is not anything that really happens (unless it is, by chance, something I also do or think in waking life), though it happens "in me"—that is, it seems to me at the time, or in recollection, that my dreamt thoughts and actions are my own.

(3)   I am responsible for doing only what is in my power to refrain from doing (since 'ought' implies 'can' and 'ought not to' implies 'can refrain from'); what I do or think in my dreams is not something it is in my power to refrain from doing or thinking.

Let us now consider each of these three responses from Augustine's point of view. In each case my questions are, Did Augustine actually offer, or even suggest, such a response? and Is Augustine entitled to offer such a response, given his views on other relevant topics?

Augustine certainly toys with response (1) when he asks, "Surely it cannot be that when I am asleep I am not myself, O Lord my God?" But who is it, if it is not I, who appears as me in my dreams? Augustine's tentative suggestion (and Plato's) is that my dream self is to be thought of as a *part* of me, perhaps some part that is left over when my reason is "sealed off" or "falls asleep with the senses of the body." The idea is reminiscent of Plato's suggestion that, whereas reason slumbers during what we call sleep, appetite, that "wild beast within us," is then awake. Plato, as we have seen, does not absolve a person of all responsibility for the exploits of the dream self. He recommends that one's reason tame the lower self before sleep, that is, before the sleep of reason, so that dream acts of passion and appetite on the loose nevertheless conform to reason.

Augustine, if he had accepted this point of view, would have had to chastise himself, not directly for the acts of his dream self, but indirectly for not preparing his appetitive and spirited selves to act on their own in conformity with reason, or at least in conformity with the "chaste resolutions" of waking life, that is, the waking life of reason. Here would be further cause to lament his lack of singlemindedness, which is a theme of Books VII and VIII of the *Confessions* ("My inner self was a house divided against itself"; VIII.8).

In the passage under consideration from Book X, however, Augustine pretty clearly backs away from response (1). First, he points out that, although reason is frequently totally absent in dreams, it is sometimes at least partially present: "And why is it that even in sleep I often resist the attractions of these images, for I remember my chaste resolutions and abide by them and give no consent to temptations of this sort?" Moreover, Augustine goes on after the part of the passage I have quoted in a manner that makes clear that he thinks he is, after all, the I* who acts, thinks, and has feelings in his dreams: "By your grace [my soul] will no longer commit in sleep these shameful, unclean acts . . . it is no great task [for you, O God] to prescribe that no temptations of this kind . . . should arouse pleasure in me, even in sleep. . . ." In fact, Augustine never, as far as I can determine—not elsewhere in the *Confessions*, not in any other work—deviates from the view that one is one*'s dream self. Here are relevant passages from *On the Soul and Its Origin,* which is quite a late work:

> For in dreams, when we suffer anything harsh and troublesome, we are, of course, still ourselves. . . . (IV.17.25)

> [The soul] never appears to itself in dreams with its own body; and yet in the very similitude of its own body it runs hither and thither through known and unknown places, and beholds many sad and joyous sights. (ibid.)

> Now when we suffer pain, if only in our dreams, although it is only the similitude of bodily limbs which is in action, and not the bodily limbs themselves, still the pain is not merely in sem-

blance, but in reality; as is also the case in the instance of joyous sensations. (IV.18.27)

Augustine also never seems to accept Plato's view that only part of one's soul is to be identified with the dream self. As he says in *The Immortality of the Soul*, "[T]hrough a bodily change such as sleep, the soul's use of the same body can be reduced, but not the soul's proper life" (14.23).

Even if Augustine never offers response (1), is he nevertheless entitled to make it? To answer that question we need to recall his concessive response to the epistemological dream problem, what I called the immunity response. According to this response, there are many things that I know, such as the fact that I am now tasting a sweet taste, even if I do not know whether I am now awake. The immunity response seems to presuppose that a pleasure, one that I have in my dream, for example, is directly experienced *by me* and known to me in exactly the way that a pleasure in waking life is experienced by me and known to me. And, since on Augustine's view I do not experience the pleasures of anyone else in this direct way, it must be that I am my dream self.

The more general point is this. Offering the immunity response to the epistemological dream problem leaves Augustine treating his dreaming that he does so-and-so as a case of its seeming to him that he really does so-and-so. To treat a dream action in this way includes treating his dream self as himself. So response (1) is not open to him.

All this bears on present-moment dream skepticism. It is the immunity response, I suggested in Chapters 5 and 7, that limits the damage posed by the threat of never knowing whether one is then dreaming. But it is precisely the immunity response that guarantees that it is I who is I* in my dreams. The immunity response thus buys epistemological gains at the price of moral liabilities.

It may be worth pointing out that even someone who denies that I am my dream self might still suppose that I am morally responsible for the nature and content of my dreams. That is, as we have already noted, Plato's position; it is also Freud's position. According to Freud, we must distinguish between the "manifest" or apparent content of our dreams and their "latent" content, that is, their meaning. Freud thinks that we are responsible for the "impulses" that are expressed in our dreams, though it would be wrong to conceive that responsibility as simply being responsible for thinking, or intending to do, what one thinks or intends to do in one's dreams. We return to Freud's position at the end of this chapter.

What about response (2)? In *The Lord's Sermon on the Mount* (I.12.33–34) Augustine comments on Jesus' warning, "Whosoever looks at a woman to lust after her, has already committed adultery with her in his heart." From what he says there, as well as from other passages, it is clear that what counts in assessing sin, according to him, is something mental and intentional. More particularly, what counts is (i) whether one is the recipient of an evil *suggestion,* (ii) whether one takes *pleasure* in contemplating the evil act or thought suggested, and finally (iii) whether one *consents* to it. The consent seems to be conceived as a sort of mental nod. Whether any particular physical action accompanies or follows these mental goings-on is either altogether irrelevant to one's sinfulness or at least clearly secondary and inessential to there being sin.

Can any or all of these three elements be present in a dream? Well, if I were not my dream self, then, even though evil were suggested to my dream self and my dream self were to take pleasure in contemplating the evil act or thought suggested and were to consent to it, still it would not be I who sinned. But, as we have seen, Augustine does not claim that I am not my dream self. On the contrary, he insists that I am my dream self, and he is not entitled to a disclaimer of identity.

Is what I do and think in my dreams anything that really happens? It seems that, on Augustine's way of thinking about dreams, dreamt suggestion, pleasure, and consent are indeed cases of suggestion, pleasure, and consent. To be sure, they take place in a dream. But their taking place when one is in a dream state no more robs them of reality than their taking place when one is in a state of agitation or depression would. And if I am my dream self, it is I who receives the evil suggestion, takes pleasure in contemplating the evil act or thought suggested, and gives consent to it.

One might try insisting that suggestion, pleasure, and consent in a dream are only apparent, not real, suggestion, pleasure, and consent. But we have already seen that Augustine in *Against the Academics* rejects the alleged distinction in reality between the pleasure of a dream and the pleasure of waking life. He must, I think, do the same thing concerning any attempted distinction between real and merely apparent suggestion.

Perhaps consent is different. One might hope to draw a distinction between real and apparent consent in such a way that the most one could do in a dream is to *seem* to oneself to consent to something. But I know of no passage in which Augustine draws such a distinction. It would go against his tendency to view the mind and its acts as directly and immediately known to itself. Moreover, in the passage we are discussing from the *Confessions*, Augustine talks about how sometimes in his dreams he remembers his "chaste resolutions" and gives "no consent to temptations of this sort." The implication is clearly that in other dreams he does give consent, real consent, and so real consent is possible in dreams. Exactly that is what one would expect Augustine to say.

It thus seems that all the elements required for a complete sin, according to Augustine, can be present, according to him, in a dream. And so the first part of response (2) is not available to him. As for the part about what I do in my dreams happening "in me," Augustine pretty clearly embraces that; it is, he says "in some way or other done in us." But Augustine's intentionalism in ethics is so strong that what counts morally is what happens "in me." What counts morally, in this case, are (i) the suggestion that I might have sex, (ii) the taking pleasure in the thought of having sex, and (iii) the inner consent to have sex. With respect to each of these three elements, there is no contrast between appearance and reality to draw, or, at least, that seems to be Augustine's view. So Augustine is not entitled to response (2). That leaves only response (3). Two contemporaries of Augustine's, the British monk Pelagius and his disciple Coelestius, made the principle that 'ought' implies 'can' a central tenet of their religious and ethical teaching. Augustine is the person primarily responsible for defining their teaching, Pelagianism, as a Christian heresy. To put a complex set of issues in their simplest terms, one could say, perhaps, that Augustine first calls for a clarification of the doctrine that

(i)   If x ought to do A, then x can do A.

Does it mean, he asks (in effect), that

(ii)   If x ought to do A, then x can do A independently of the gratuitous assistance (i.e., grace) of God.

Or does it mean that

(iii)   If x ought to do A, then x can do A, though perhaps only with the gratuitous assistance (i.e., grace) of God.

Augustine rejects (ii) and brands it the heresy, "Pelagianism," though he accepts (iii).

One implication of these points is brought out in the following quotation from Augustine's *On Man's Perfection in Righteousness* (a treatise that in some manuscripts carries the subtitle *In opposition to those who assert that it is possible for a man to become righteous by his own sole strength* and in one manuscript carries the subtitle *A treatise on what are called the definitions of*

Coelestius): "Why should that be commanded which cannot at all be done? The answer is, that man is most wisely commanded to walk with right steps, on purpose that, when he has discovered his own inability to do even this, he may seek the remedy which is provided for the inward man to cure the lameness of sin, even the grace of God, through our Lord Jesus Christ" (III.6).

With the difference between (ii) and (iii) in mind, let us consider now these two amplifications of response (3):

(3′)   I am responsible for doing only what is in my power, unaided by the gratuitous assistance of God, to refrain from doing; what I do or think in my dreams is not something that it is in my power, unaided by the grace of God, to refrain from doing or thinking.

(3″)   I am responsible for doing only what is in my power, together with the gratuitous assistance of God, to refrain from doing; what I do or think in my dreams is not something that it is in my power, together with the gratuitous assistance of God, to refrain from doing or thinking.

Augustine can be expected to reject the first half of (3′) and the second half of (3″). Indeed, what Augustine goes on to say in the latter half of the chapter from the *Confessions* with which we began confirms these expectations:

> The power of your hand, O God almighty, is indeed great enough to cure all the diseases of my soul. By granting me more abundant grace you can even quench the fire of sensuality which provokes me in my sleep. . . . By your grace [my soul] will no longer commit in sleep these shameful, unclean acts inspired by sensual images, which lead to the pollution of the body: it will not so much as consent to them. (X.30)

Thus Augustine pretty clearly rejects response (3). And, in view of his adamant anti-Pelagianism, we can say that he is not entitled to (3) anyway.

In summary, we have seen that Augustine rejects each of the three responses I have suggested might absolve him of all responsibility for what he does and thinks in his dreams. Moreover, he is not, given other views he holds, entitled to any of the three. Unless I have ignored some appropriate response, Augustine is not justified in saying, as he does in the middle of the chapter I have been concentrating on, "Yet the difference between waking and sleeping is so great that even when, during sleep, it happens otherwise [i.e., when during sleep I consent to have sex], I return to a clear conscience when I wake and realize that, because of this difference, I was not responsible for the act." In fact, he has no way to understand the difference between waking and sleeping that justifies his putatively clear conscience. Moreover, one judges from the rest of the chapter that his conscience is not really as clear as he would like to think it is.[1]

In Book XII of *The Literal Meaning of Genesis*, Augustine makes his most determined effort to escape responsibility for unchaste dreams. He first maintains that nocturnal emissions are simply a natural reaction to sexually provocative dream

---

1. Perhaps I should say that *I* judge this. Other readers may gain a different impression. Gerard O'Daly says flatly, "For Augustine . . . responsibility in dreams cannot be admitted; our will is not sovereign"; see *Augustine's Philosophy of Mind* (Berkeley: University of California Press, 1987), 116. But O'Daly cites no direct evidence for his claim, and he does not deal with the reasoning I present in discussing response (3) above. Moreover, he adds this: "At the same time, Augustine is not unaffected by the belief, common in antiquity among philosophers, that our dreams somehow reflect our moral character"; ibid., 117.

William E. Mann, who seems to share my assessment of Augustine's concern about the problem, as well as my judgment about the problem's independent interest, offers this as one way of viewing Augustine's own ambivalence: Augustine "is not convinced that he is responsible for his dreams, but neither is he convinced that he is not. His vacillation *can* be viewed as a case of a philosopher's being forced to accept an unpalatable consequence of his philosophical doctrines, in which case the uncertainty can be explained solely in terms of the logical tensions between the various philosophical components and the deliverances of common sense." Mann goes on to insist that the problem remains even "after we tinker with the components"; see "Dreams of Immorality," *Philosophy* 58 (1983), 384.

images. He then insists that one cannot even speak of carnal intercourse, and mean what one says, without having unchaste images before one's mind. "Moreover," he goes on, "when the image that arises in the thoughts of the speaker becomes so vivid in the dream of the sleeper that it is indistinguishable from actual intercourse, it immediately moves the flesh and the natural result follows. Yet this happens without sin, just as the matter is spoken of without sin by a man wide awake, who doubtless thinks about it in order to speak of it" (XII.15.31).

This effort is unconvincing. Perhaps there is nothing sinful, even in Augustine's own terms, about having a lewd dream that produces a nocturnal emission. But what about Augustine's three elements of sin—suggestion, pleasure, and consent? If—in the dream—one finds a lewd image that is suggestive, one takes pleasure in the suggestion of intercourse, and one consents to intercourse, then surely there is sin. Even if there is only suggestion, there is the root of sin. Thus, what Augustine exonerates—the nocturnal emission following a lewd dream image—is different from what, in his own terms, would incriminate him, namely, a suggestion within in the dream of the possibility of having intercourse.

&

Among the various commitments that rule out, for Augustine, responses (1–3), it is doubtless the anti-Pelagianism that readers find the least appealing.[2] In turning now to Descartes's response to the moral dream problem, we have a chance to consider whether response (3) might be available to a Cartesian who does not share Augustine's anti-Pelagianism.

2. Although, as William E. Mann points out, all we need from Augustine's anti-Pelagianism to make the moral dream problem a serious one is "scepticism about the universal applicability of the principle that 'ought' implies 'can.'" As Mann goes on to remark, that principle, "like many other principles of similar generality, wobbles between being made trivially true on the one hand and being patently false on the other"; "Dreams of Immortality," 379.

The major problem with (3), I think, is that of justifying the claim that what I do or think in my dreams is not something that it is in my power to refrain from doing or thinking. Justifying that claim is particularly hard for a Cartesian, in view of the fact that Descartes says this about free will in Meditation IV:

> It is only the will, or freedom of choice, which I experience within me to be so great that the idea of any greater faculty is beyond my grasp; . . . For although God's will is incomparably greater than mine, . . . nevertheless it does not seem any greater than mine when considered as will in the essential and strict sense. This is because the will simply consists in our ability to do or not do something (that is, to affirm or deny, to pursue or avoid); or rather, it consists simply in the fact that when the intellect puts something forward for affirmation or denial or for pursuit or avoidance, our inclinations are such that we do not *feel* we are determined by any external force. In order to be free, there is no need for me to be inclined both ways. (AT VII, 57; CSM II, 40, emphasis added)

It is hard to see how, given this understanding of what freedom of the will consists in, one could be sure that what one does in one's dreams is never done of one's own free will and therefore is never something it is in one's power to refrain from doing.[3] It comes, then, as something of a surprise to find that Descartes, in the only passage I know of in which he discusses the moral dream problem, says this:

> For everybody wants to make himself happy; but most people do not know how to, and often a bodily indisposition prevents their will from being free. This happens too when we are

3. Consider Descartes's letter to Reneri for Pollot (April 1638): "It does not seem to me a fiction, but a truth which nobody should deny, that there is nothing entirely in our power except our thoughts; at least if you take the word 'thought' as I do, to cover all operations of the soul, . . . not only meditations and acts of will. . . ." (K, 51). But see also the latter to Mersenne, 3 December 1640 (K, 84).

asleep; because nobody, however philosophical, can prevent himself having bad dreams when his temperament disposes him. However, experience shows that if one has often had a certain thought while one's mind was at liberty, it returns again however indisposed one's body may be. Thus I can boast that my own dreams never portray anything distressing, and there is no doubt that it is a great advantage to have long accustomed oneself to drive away sad thought. But we cannot altogether answer for ourselves except when we are in our own power. (Letter to Elizabeth, 1 September 1645; K, 167–68)

When Descartes says that "we cannot altogether answer for ourselves except when we are in our own power," I take him to imply, given the context, that we are not in our own power when we dream, and that therefore we cannot altogether answer for dream thoughts and actions. But given Descartes's account of free will in Meditation IV, there seems to be no reason to say that one never has free will in one's dreams. On Descartes's account, to say that one was free in a dream would only be to say that in the dream one could affirm, deny, pursue, or avoid something without *feeling* any external force.

A defender of Descartes might want to try the following line of defense. Although one can indeed affirm, deny, pursue, or avoid something in a dream without any feeling of external force, to do that is only to dream that one affirms, denies, and so on and only to dream that one feels no external force. I cannot see, though, that there is any support for such a move in Descartes himself. Descartes seems to hold that dreaming one affirms something is a genuine case of affirming something, and dreaming that one affirms something without any feeling of external force would be for him, it seems, a genuine case of doing that without any feeling of external force. If I am right about this, the moral dream problem poses for Descartes, too, the 'I*' question, 'Am I morally responsible for what I* do and think in my dreams?' He answers "no," but without adequate justification—at least

if we can hold him to his account of free will in Meditation
IV.[4]

As we have seen, Augustine takes seriously the 'I*' question,
'Am I morally responsible for what I* think and do in my
dreams?' One should not forget, however, that even someone
who denies that I am my dream self and, for that reason,
objects to this 'I*' question may yet suppose that I am responsible for the *content* of my dreams. That is, as I have already
pointed out, Freud's position.

Freud thinks we are responsible for the "impulses" that are
expressed in our dreams; they are, he thinks, our very own
impulses, even though it would be a mistake to think of our
responsibility as being accountable for what the dream self
does, since we are not our dream self. Here is a striking pas-

4. It is Spinoza, rather than Descartes, who takes with full seriousness the
assertion that what I do in my dreams is not done freely. But instead of
supporting this claim with an argument, he uses it as a supposition and,
agreeing with Descartes that there are no certain signs to distinguish dreams
from waking life, he argues for the conclusion that what I do in my waking
life is not free either: "[W]hen we dream that we are speaking, we think that
we do so from free mental decision; yet we are not speaking, or if we are, it is
the result of spontaneous movement of the body. Again, we dream that we
are keeping something secret, and that we are doing so by the same mental
decision that comes into play in our waking hours when we keep silent about
what we know. Finally, we dream that from a mental decision we act as we
dare not act when awake. So I would very much like to know whether in the
mind there are two sorts of decisions, dreamland decisions and free decisions. If we don't want to carry madness so far, we must necessarily grant that
the mental decision that is believed to be free is not distinct from imagination
and memory. . . . So these mental decisions arise in the mind from the same
necessity as the ideas of things existing in actuality, and those who believe that
they speak, or keep silent, or do anything from free mental decision are
dreaming with their eyes open." Baruch Spinoza, *Ethics and Selected Letters*,
trans. Samuel Shirley (Indianapolis: Hackett, 1982). For a discussion of Spinoza on the moral dream problem, see Harold Zellner, "Spinoza's Puzzle,"
History of Philosophy Quarterly 5 (1988), 233–43.

sage from an addendum to his famous *Interpretation of Dreams* titled "Moral Responsibility for the Content of Dreams":

> If I seek to classify the impulses that are present in me according to social standards into good and bad, I must assume responsibility for both sorts; and if, in defense, I say that what is unknown, unconscious and repressed in me is not my 'ego,' then I shall not be basing my position upon psycho-analysis, I shall not have accepted its conclusions and I shall perhaps be taught better by the criticisms of my fellowmen, by the disturbances in my actions and the confusion of my feelings. I shall perhaps learn that what I am repudiating not only 'is' in me but sometimes 'acts' from out of me as well.[5]

It is interesting that, in insisting that we have moral responsibility for the content of our dreams, Freud at the same time warns us that the ego is not as isolated as we might like to think.

5. Sigmund Freud, *Collected Papers*, trans. James Strachey (New York: Basic Books, 1959), 5:154–57.

[9]

The Problem of Other Minds

It is sometimes assumed that the problem of other minds (How do I know that there are minds associated with other human bodies, when all I can ever observe directly are bodies and bodily actions, or perhaps even only bodily appearances?) is one of those endlessly perplexing problems we owe to Descartes. Some people suppose, not only that this problem is stated by him, but also that it is answered by him with the argument from analogy.[1] Accordingly, I infer the existence of other minds by extrapolating from the correlation I can observe between by own mental states, which I know directly, and certain actions of my own body; I extrapolate that that correlation holds as well between mental states

1. Thus Gilbert Ryle, in *The Concept of Mind* (London: Hutchinson's Library, 1949), 14, includes this in his account of what he calls "Descartes' Myth": " . . . one person has no direct access of any sort to the events of the inner life of another. He cannot do better than make problematic inferences from the observed behaviour of the other person's body to the states of mind which, by analogy from his own conduct, he supposes to be signalised by that behaviour." In a much more scholarly discussion, Donald F. Henze tries to say what form a Cartesian argument for other minds would take, if Descartes were to have offered one. For this purpose he reconstructs "an argument somewhat like that from analogy"; see "Descartes on Other Minds," *Studies in the Philosophy of Mind* (American Philosophical Quarterly Monograph Series, no. 6, 1972), 54.

of others, which I cannot know directly, and the actions of other human bodies that, as I can see, resemble actions of my own body.

It is natural enough to expect Descartes to have stated the problem of other minds. Reconstructing knowledge as he does from his foundation stone, 'I am', he is surely faced with this problem. After all, he insists that the mind is a purely thinking thing that is unextended, that is, nonspatial, and hence unobservable to the bodily senses. So how *do* we know that other human bodies are not just complex robots, with no "mental inside" to them?

Does Descartes actually state the problem of other minds? And, if he does, does he offer the argument from analogy as its solution? The most natural place to look for an answer to those questions is in Descartes's rational reconstruction of knowledge, just after he has told us what a mind is, in the last part of Meditation II. The closest thing one finds to a statement of the problem there is this passage:

> We say that we see the wax itself, if it is there before us, not that we judge it to be there from its colour or shape; and this might lead me to conclude without more ado that knowledge of the wax comes from what the eye sees, and not from the scrutiny of the mind alone [*visione oculi, non solius mentis inspectione*]. But then if I look out of the window and see men crossing the square, as I just happen to have done, I normally say that I see the men themselves, just as I say that I see the wax. Yet do I see any more than hats and coats which could conceal automatons? I *judge* that they are men. And so something which I thought I was seeing with my eyes is in fact grasped solely by the faculty of judgement which is in my mind. (AT VII, 32; CSM II, 21)

Is this a statement of the problem of other minds? Many people seem to have thought so. There is certainly a contrast here between what one sees to be the case and what one judges to be the case. That reminds us of the contrast that underlies the problem of other minds between what can be observed directly (bodies, perhaps—or perhaps only the appearances of bodies—and one's own mind, but certainly not other minds) and what is only inferred. So far, so good. We have just had in the immediately preceding discussion the example of a piece of wax that has lost all the perceptible qualities it formerly had. It is not that it now has no perceptible qualities at all; rather, each perceptible quality it formerly had has now gone, but there are now certain other perceptible qualities instead. Descartes then makes the point that one cannot tell "from what the eye sees [*visione oculi*]" that it is the same wax in a new state, though one can make the judgment by "mental inspection." The hats-and-coats analogy is meant to underline this contrast between what one can see by "ocular vision" and what requires mental inspection. Thus one cannot actually see with the eyes that there are human beings under those hats and cloaks, though one may judge by mental inspection that there are.

It is worth emphasizing that Descartes does *not* say, as one might have expected him to, that he does not see minds, or thoughts, within those bodies; rather, he says that one does not see while looking "out of the window" that these are men, human beings, under those hats and cloaks, rather than concealed automata. Judgment must take over because the eyes, from the window anyway, cannot rule out this possibility:

(P_1) There are not men under the hats and cloaks, but only automata.

To get the problem of other minds going, one would need to introduce the suggestion that, even if we went down onto the street and rudely disrobed and dehatted those decorous figures, we could still not rule out, "from what the eyes see," this possibility:

(P_2) There are no minds to go with those human bodies.

The worry about how to rule out (P$_2$) is not excluded by the text, but it goes well beyond it. There is no explicit suggestion in the text of a worry that could not be dispelled by taking off the hats and coats, or perhaps simply by peeking discretely under them. Without a worry about how I can be justified in inferring that there are other minds, when the only one I can observe directly is my own, there is no problem of other minds.

I can imagine someone protesting that my reading of the hats-and-coats passage is superficial. After all, Descartes has before him the case of the oderless, colorless, tasteless, virtually inaudible liquid that is the product of melting down a piece of sweet-smelling, milky-looking, and solid-enough-sounding wax. His point is that one cannot *see* the liquid stuff to be the same; one *judges* it to be so. It is no accidental, or remediable, circumstance that prevents us from making the identification by "ocular vision." The persistence of a sensible substance through a change in all its sensible properties cannot be observed; *in principle* it cannot be observed. The disappearance of the first set of properties can be observed, as can the appearance of the new, and in this case rather more modest, set, but not the persistence of the substance through this total exchange in perceptible qualities.

Now, if that is Descartes's example, and it certainly is, and he moves to illuminate it by the hats-and-coats case, as he certainly does, surely the illuminating example should not be one in which what blocks seeing that *p* is simply some accidental circumstance, such as the temporary obstruction of one's view by hats and cloaks. Surely, if the example is to be apposite to Descartes's purpose, one should be unable in principle to see that these are human beings. Therefore, what is at stake must be whether these bodies have *minds* to go with them, or whether, alternatively, they are only automata.

No doubt it has been exegetical reasoning like this that has led people to suppose that the problem of other minds must be what is at stake in the hats-and-coats passage in Meditation

II. The fact remains that Descartes never actually states this problem there, or, as far as I can discover, anywhere else. No doubt he sets things up in a way that encourages us to state the problem for ourselves, but that is the most one can say.

So here is my judicious verdict on the hats-and-coats passage. To a reader today it may indeed suggest the problem of other minds. But Descartes does not himself pose the problem here, or elsewhere. In this passage he is making a point about how we may be misled by ordinary language. "I am almost tricked by ordinary ways of talking," he writes. "We say that we see the wax itself, if it is there before us, not that we judge it to be there from its colour or shape" (AT VII, 32; CSM II, 21). But, as his thought experiment has just brought out, the wax may undergo a complete change of perceptible qualities, so that the most we can do is "judge it to be there from [seeing] its colour or shape."

By way of analogy, Descartes points out that we are also inclined to say that we *see* men crossing the square when, for all we can actually see, what we see might actually be automata that are covered by hats and coats. Just as in that case, what we really do is judge those figures to be human beings, so in the wax case, what we really do is judge the stuff before us to be wax.

To us this passage may indeed suggest the question, How do we get from what we really see, or directly observe (e.g., things like hats and coats, or perhaps more basically, bodies and their movements, or even more austerely, shapes and patches of color), to what we judge or infer (e.g., that those figures are human beings, creatures with minds)? This passage may even suggest to us, as a reply to the problem of other minds, some version of the argument from analogy—perhaps this: it is by noting the similarity between movements of those bodies and certain movements of my own body with which I have previously correlated mental contents that I may infer that there are similar mental contents, and hence minds, associated with those hatted and coated bodies. Descartes, however, raises no such question. Nor does he provide any such answer. He does not ask how one can know that there is another mind, in addition to one's own. He simply insists that one judges, rather than sees, that those are human beings, creatures with minds, and not automata.

☙

Although the problem of other minds is not raised explicitly anywhere in Descartes, it is raised, it seems, in Augustine. Indeed, it looks as though Augustine seeks to solve it with the argument from analogy:

> For we also recognize, from a likeness to us, the motions of bodies by which we perceive that others besides us live. Just as we move [our] body in living, so, we notice, those bodies are moved. For when a living body is moved there is no way open to our eyes to see the mind [*animus*], a thing which cannot be seen by the eyes. But we perceive something present in that mass such as is present in us to move our mass in a similar way; it is life and soul [*anima*]. Nor is such perception something peculiar to, as it were, human prudence and reason. For indeed beasts perceive as living, not only themselves, but also each other and one another, and us as well. Nor do they see our soul [*animas*], except from the motions of the body, and they do that immediately and very simply by a sort of natural agreement. Therefore we know the mind of anyone at all from our own; and from our own case we believe in that which we do not know [*ex nostro credimus quem non novimus*]. For not only do we perceive a mind, but we even know what one is, by considering our own; for we have a mind. (*Trinity*, VIII.6.9, author's trans.)

On first reading, anyway, this passage seems to suggest that Augustine realizes that the problem of other minds is a serious problem for anyone with his (and, as it turns out, Descartes's) first-person orientation in philosophy and his belief that minds are nonspatial entities. If this is right, then Augustine is already, it seems, a step ahead of Descartes. Moreover, Augustine seems to offer in this passage, as a response to the problem of other minds, the very argument that recent philosophers have taken to be the natural Cartesian response, namely, the argument from analogy. Since the argument from analogy is not to be found in Descartes either, Augustine seems, again, to be far ahead of his time.

Natural as this assessment of the situation is, it is also, I think, quite wrong.[2] To see why it is wrong, let us turn back to Descartes. The problem of other minds assumes a first-person starting point in philosophy, from which one then asks how one knows that there is a mind besides one's own ("How do I know that there are minds in addition to the one I* have?"). The first-person starting point, as we have seen, is certainly Cartesian. From Descartes's example, modern philosophers have learned to undertake for themselves a rational reconstruction of knowledge and to do it from a first-person beginning. Though Descartes does eventually, in the final Meditation, undertake to solve the problem of the external world, he never, as I have urged in this chapter, takes on the problem of other minds. If, however, we use Part V of the *Discourse* to flesh out Descartes's thinking on the external world, we can easily come up with something at least germane to the problem of other minds. There Descartes occupies himself with the question of which entities have minds. His first concern is over how we might recognize that even cleverly constructed robots are not human beings. He offers two tests: one is language, the other is a certain adaptability through reason ("reason is a universal instrument . . . [whereas] these organs [of the machines] need a particular

2. The interpretation I say is natural on first reading is actually one I held after many readings. In a seminar paper he wrote for me many years ago at the University of Minnesota, T. Michael McNulty first gave me second thoughts about my reading of the passage. McNulty later argued for his own interpretation in his "Augustine's Argument for the Existence of Other Souls," *Modern Schoolman* 48 (1970), 19–25.

disposition for each particular action . . .") (AT VI, 57; CSM I, 140). By means of these two tests, Descartes goes on to say, we can distinguish human beings from beasts.

It soon becomes clear in this section of the *Discourse* that what Descartes is interested in here is the possession of a rational mind, or soul. Thus the two tests he offers to mark off human beings from both the most cleverly constructed robots and the most humanlike beasts are really tests for whether something has a mind. To bring into focus just what Descartes attempts to show about other minds, and what he does not, it is important to distinguish these claims:

(A) There are minds in addition to my own.
(B) That individual over there has a mind.
(C) Each functional individual of kind *k* has a mind.
(D) Some functional individuals of kind *k* have minds.

The modern problem of other minds takes its form against the background assumption that the rational reconstruction of knowledge requires that (A) be justified, if at all, as a generalization from (B)-type claims. The point of the argument from analogy is to establish a (B)-type claim and, by that means, to establish (A) itself. Descartes himself, however, shows no special interest in establishing (A). It is not that he rejects it, or even thinks it questionable. Certainly he thinks it true. What he is primarily concerned about, however, are (C)-type claims. He accepts this one:

(C_1) Each functional individual of kind *human* has a mind.

Maintaining in Part V of the *Discourse* that "there are no men so dull-witted or stupid—and this includes even madmen— that they are incapable of arranging various words together and forming an utterance from them in order to make their thoughts understood" (AT VI, 57; CSM 1, 140), Descartes seeks to support (C_1) by use of the language test.

Descartes rejects this (C)-type claim:

(C_2) Each functional individual of kind *animal* has a mind.

All nonhuman animals, he supposes, fail both the language test and the adaptability test and can thus be shown to lack minds.
Moreover, Descartes rejects this (D)-type claim:

(D_1) Some individuals of kind *automaton* have minds.

Again, his reasoned basis for rejecting (D_1) is that all automata fail both tests for having a mind.
Concentrating on the language test, and ignoring the adaptability test, we have these three arguments so far:
Argument 1:

(1)   Each language user has a mind. (language test, first half)
(2)   Each functional individual of kind *human* is a language user.

Therefore,

(3)   Each functional individual of kind *human* has a mind. (C_1)

Argument 2:

(4)   Only language users have minds. (language test, second half)
(5)   Not all functional individuals of kind *animal* are language users.

Therefore,

(6)   Not all functional individuals of kind *animal* have minds. (denial of C_2)

Argument 3:

(7)   Only language users have minds. (language test, second half)
(8)   No individual of kind *automaton* is a language user.

Therefore,

(9)   No individual of kind *automaton* has a mind. (denial of D_1)

As for (A), it is clearly available to Descartes by a valid argument from

(10) There are several functional individuals of kind *human*,

together with the conclusion of Argument 1 above, namely, (3). (To be more precise, what one gets is 'There are several minds'. One then needs to add the assumption, 'If there are several minds, there are minds in addition to my own'.)

By the time Descartes gets to Part V of the *Discourse* (Part IV contains in summary form much of the rational reconstruction of knowledge that is spread throughout the six Meditations), he certainly thinks he has good reason to accept (10). So he has available to him, as he would suppose, a very good basis for accepting (A), that is, for thinking that there are indeed minds other than his own.

In summary, Descartes shows no special interest in establishing (A). But by the time he gets to Part V of the *Discourse*, he clearly accepts premises (1, 2, and 10) that place it comfortably beyond doubt. Moreover, that line of argumentation is independent of, and, I should have thought, quite superior to, the argument from analogy.

Is it not only superior but also good? If 'language user' is interpreted strictly enough to make (1) plausible, then (2) seems false, or at the very least suspect. But if we change the 'all' in (2) to 'several', then the result is surely acceptable; and we have an even simpler argument for (A), namely this one:

Argument 4:

(11) Each language user has a mind. (language test, first half)

(12) Several functional individuals of kind *human* are language users.

Therefore,

(13) Several functional individuals of kind *human* have minds.

Therefore,

(14) There are several minds.

(15) If there are several minds, there are minds in addition to my own.

Therefore,

(16) There are minds in addition to my own. (A)

Here is surely a better way of dealing with the problem of other minds than any that makes essential use of the argument from analogy. And it is quite honestly Cartesian, even though it is not stated in so many words by Descartes himself.

Someone might object that my reconstruction of Descartes is entirely inappropriate. After all, I explained the problem of other minds as something that begins with a contrast between what one can observe directly and what must be inferred. The problem then takes shape from the thought that other minds cannot be observed directly; at most it is human bodies, perhaps only the appearances of human bodies, that can be observed directly. The question is then how one can be justified in inferring, on the basis of what one observes directly, that there exist other minds.

I have maintained that Descartes's best response to the problem of other minds is an argument from other language users. But surely whether x is a genuine language user is not something that can be observed directly; it must be inferred from the actions and noise emissions of some body. So either the solution I have given Descartes is an *ignoratio elenchi* because it ignores the problem altogether or else it is ineffective because it does not show how the existence of other minds may be inferred from properties that are directly observable.

Here is my reply. Certainly the argument I have reconstructed from Descartes does not seek to establish the existence of other minds as an inference from directly observable properties. But that is in its favor. To attempt to establish the existence of other minds as an inference from evidence of directly observable properties is rather like trying to establish that there exist noncounterfeit coins by producing some examples and defending the proposition that those particular coins, or perhaps even any coins with specified observable properties that those coins share, could not possibly be counterfeit. One knows that there are noncounterfeit coins, not by knowing that this one is certainly, beyond all possibility of even hyperbolical doubt, noncounterfeit, and that that one is too, but rather by knowing that there are governments that have set up mints that have produced genuine coins. One can know that that is all true without ever being in a position to produce a single coin that could not possibly turn out, on later inspection, or on further investigation, to be counterfeit.

So it is with other language users. Perhaps a computer program can be written that will make it impossible for me to determine whether or not there is a human being on the other end of my telephone connection. Some day a thoroughly convincing robot may instantiate such a program. But such a possibility does nothing to impugn facts about human societies that place beyond reasonable doubt the proposition that there are other language users. For the knowledge that there are other language users does not rest on an induction from specific cases. Thus the argument I have reconstructed from Descartes is a good response to the problem of other minds. And part of the reason it is a good response is that it begins from another starting point altogether.

I can imagine someone still resisting my claim that the argument from other language users is superior to the argument from analogy. It is small comfort, my objector will insist, to be told that

(12)   Several functional individuals of kind *human* are language users.

need not be established by proving that this individual is a language user (in an appropriately strong sense of 'language user') and that that one is, and so on. Claims about large groups of people are no less open, than are claims about individuals, to the kind of hyperbolical skepticism that leads Descartes in Meditation I to suppose that "the heavens, the air, the earth, colours, shapes, sounds and all external things that we see, are only illusions and deceptions" and that he has "no hands, eyes, flesh, blood or senses" at all but only mistakenly believes that he has those things.

The objection is significant but not, I think, devastating. Perhaps one has no general knowledge of there being language users that stands up to the hyperbolical doubt of Meditation I. But we should remember that Descartes does not attempt to prove even the existence of the external world without appeal to the existence and nature of God. When he gets around to proving that there exists an external world, in Meditation VI, he argues that God, being no deceiver, "has permitted no falsity in my opinions which he has not also given me some faculty capable of correcting." Since he has no faculty for correcting his belief that there exists an external world and, indeed, a strong inclination to believe that there is one, that belief, he supposes, is true.

Similar reasoning applies to skepticism about other language users. The belief that I am now confronted by another language user is something I might be mistaken about in a way that I do have a "faculty" for correcting. For example, I might question my "conversation" partner in such a way as to expose the fact that its responses are all programmed. By contrast, the belief that there simply exist other language users is of an entirely different order. How could it be the case that I, alone, use a language that others only parrot? The belief that there simply exist other language users, unlike the belief that there is one at the other end of the telephone line, or across the desk from me, is a belief that I have no faculty for correcting. Since I have a strong, indeed an overwhelming, inclination to accept it, and no faculty for correcting it, it must, by Descartes's reasoning, be true.

The supposition that only I am a genuine language user would presumably include the idea that words have no meaning independent of the meaning I assign them. To take such a supposition seriously invites the most horrendous worries about whether my words, and even the thoughts "behind" my words, really succeed in picking things out or describing anything picked out. It seems that Descartes rather deliberately excludes basic worries about language and meaning from the domain of systematic doubt. It is hard to see how, if basic doubts about language were let in, there could be room for confidence that Descartes could even formulate or apply his method of systematic doubt. Does that mean that certain basic assumptions are kept immune to the force of the systematic doubt? I think it does. But it is good to think that reasoning similar to his proof of the external world might at least give ex post facto justification to this policy of selective immunity. In any case, it is well to keep in mind that the method of systematic doubt does not require that one exhaust all possible objects of doubt. The method requires only that one undertake to reject everything dubitable *until* one comes up with something indubitable.

֍

Earlier I suggested that, on first examination, it seems to be Augustine rather that Descartes who presents the problem of other minds and offers the argument from analogy as its solution. I went on to argue that first appearances are, in this case, deceiving. The point of the passage I quoted from Augustine's *Trinity* is in fact rather different from anything we have considered so far. It has to do, not with the limits of what one can *know*, but rather with the limits of what one might *believe* to exist. Augustine wants to explain how it ever occurs to us (or to beasts, for that matter) to attribute minds, or souls, to other beings.

Augustine's problem of other minds can be thought of as a problem about meaning. "For who, upon reading or listening to the writings of Paul the Apostle, or of those . . . written about him, does not draw a picture in his mind of the countenance of the Apostle himself, and of all those whose names are there mentioned?" Augustine asks. Understanding the words "Paul the Apostle" includes, Augustine thinks, making a mental picture of Paul. Among the many people who read about Paul and his associates, Augustine goes on, "one represents the features and figures of those bodies in one way, and another in a different way. . . . But our faith is not busied there with the bodily countenance of those men, but only with the life that they led through the grace of God" (*Trinity,* VIII.4.7). Two chapters later Augustine comes back to Paul:

> Return, therefore, with me, and let us consider why we love the Apostle. Is it on account of his human form which is most familiar to us, because we believe him to have been a man? Certainly not; otherwise, we would have no reason for loving him now, since he is no longer that man, for his soul has been separated from his body. But we believe that what we love in him lives even now, for we love his just soul. (VIII.6.9)

The problem for Augustine is how to understand the word 'soul' (or 'mind') as a general term. But equally it is how to conceive, as a general thing, what a soul or mind is. As we note again in Chapter 12, Augustine moves easily back and forth between asking, where *t* is a general term for *f*'s, how he knows what *t* means and asking how he knows what an *f* is. That is certainly true in the passage under consideration. His problem is equally how he knows what '*anima*' (or '*animus*') means and how he knows what an *anima* or *animus* is.

Augustine's explanation of how one can know these things incorporates his version of the argument from analogy. We notice, he says, the similarity between the movements of other bodies and those of our own body. We then attribute to another body a soul, which, as we suppose, moves it much as we "observe" that our own soul moves our own body.[3] In attributing a mind or soul to another body, we make a representation, he supposes, from the direct acquaintance we have with our own mind or soul. We know the mind of any other person, he says, from our own (*animum . . . cuiuslibet ex nostro novimus*). And from our own case, he adds, we postulate, or believe in, that which we do not know, that is, that which we

---

3. ". . . [A] living man, whose soul we do not indeed see, but conjecture from our own [*ex nostra conicimus*], and from corporeal motions gaze also in thought upon the living man, as we have learnt him by sight" (*Trinity,* XIII.1.3).

are not acquainted with ourselves (*ex nostro credimus quem non novimus*). Attributing a mind to another is thus, according to Augustine, an act of postulation, or belief, not an act of knowledge.[4]

The problem of other minds, as it is usually conceived in modern philosophy, takes shape against the background of something like Descartes's method of systematic doubt and his rational reconstruction of knowledge. Thus the difference between what we can perceive *directly* (bodies, say, or perhaps only bodily appearances) and what must be inferred from what we perceive directly is important because what we can perceive directly is considered immune to doubt. The idea is that, if we can show the existence of other minds to be a warranted inference from *indubitabilia,* we will have reconstructed, rationally, our knowledge that there exist other minds.

Augustine, as we have seen, does not undertake the rational reconstruction of knowledge or follow the method of systematic doubt. He uses Cartesian-sounding arguments to defeat global skepticism, but never in the service of any general reconstruction project. Since the Cartesian project and method are missing from Augustine, and, moreover, since Augustine does not even claim to *know* (as opposed to believe) that there exist other minds, one cannot expect him to formulate the problem of other minds, or the argument from analogy, in their now customary forms.

Suppose Augustine had offered the argument from analogy, not just in response to the question, 'How do I come to believe that there are minds in addition to the one I* have?'

---

4. "For it is not said to the mind: 'Know thyself,' as it is said: 'Know the Cherubim and the Seraphim!' For they are absent, and we believe what we have been taught concerning them, that they are certain heavenly powers. Nor as it is said: 'Know the will of that man!' It is utterly impossible for us either to perceive or to understand his will unless he makes it known by some corporeal signs, and even then we believe rather than understand" (*Trinity* X.9.12).

but rather to 'How do I *know* that there are minds in addition to the one I* have?' Still, he would not, I think, have bettered Descartes on that score. Or at least he would not have offered a better response than Descartes had clearly available to him. For Descartes, as I have argued, had ready for himself a much more effective response to the problem of other minds than the argument from analogy—the argument from other language users. A version of that argument withstands critical examination and recommends itself to us as well.

[10]

Descartes's Internalism

In Part I of the *Discourse*, Descartes tells us about making a resolution on leaving school "to seek no knowledge other than that which could be found in myself or else in the great book of the world." What he understood by "seeking knowledge in the great book of the world" and why he thought that part of his project important are suggested in these lines:

> I spent the rest of my youth travelling, visiting courts and armies, mixing with people of diverse temperaments and ranks, gathering various experiences, testing myself in situations which fortune offered me, and at all times reflecting upon whatever came my way so as to derive some profit from it. For it seemed to me that much more truth could be found in the reasonings which a man makes concerning matters that concern him than in those which some scholar makes in his study about speculative matters. (AT VI, 9; CSM I, 115)

Having pursued for several years his interest in the "great book of the world," Descartes turned inward. As he puts it, "I resolved one day to undertake studies within myself too." It is this turning inward, this "undertaking studies within myself," that I now focus on.

In Part II of the *Discourse*, Descartes seems to want to justify his resolution to undertake studies within himself. One consideration he thinks important is that buildings produced by several craftsmen, or designed by more than one architect, are, as a rule, less perfect than those produced by only one. Warming to the building metaphor, he suggests that, just as it is better to raze a building and start over with new foundations, so it would be better in his own pursuit of knowledge to get rid of old opinions and "replace them afterwards with better ones, or with the same ones once I had squared them with the standards of reason" (AT VI, 13–4; CSM II, 117).

There lurks in this section, however, a line of argument for a first-person project in philosophy that is much more interesting than any appeal to the analogy of a craftsman or architect. Part of that reasoning is a claim that "in my college days I discovered that nothing can be imagined which is too strange or incredible to have been said by some philosopher." The reasoning ends with this sentence: "I was, then, unable to choose anyone whose opinions struck me as preferable to those of all others, and I found myself as it were forced to become my own guide" (AT VI, 16; CSM I, 119).

A paragraph earlier Descartes had identified a class of people who "have enough reason or modesty to recognize that they are less capable of distinguishing the true from the false than certain others by whom they can be taught." Descartes says of these people that they "should be content to follow the opinions of these others rather than seek better opinions themselves" (AT VI, 15; CSM I, 118). He adds that he would himself have been counted among these people if he "had had only one teacher or had never known the differences that have always existed among the opinions of the most learned" (AT VI, 16; CSM I, 118). From this section it is possible to construct the following argument for epistemic individualism:

(1)   Either I should become my own guide in seeking knowledge or else I should simply accept the opinions of some teacher.

(2) If I should simply accept the opinions of some teacher, then either I have only one teacher or else I do not know that differences of opinion exist among the most learned teachers.

(3) I have more than one teacher.

(4) I know that differences of opinion exist among the most learned teachers.

Therefore,

(5) I should not simply accept the opinions of some teacher.

Therefore,

(6) I should become my own guide in seeking knowledge.

   This line of reasoning will strike the thoughtful reader as, to say the least, somewhat simplistic. Consider (2). Surely one might realize that "differences of opinion exist among the most learned teachers" and yet find a way to select among them so as to be able to accept, reasonably, the opinions of one of them or perhaps the convergent set of some few. These three maxims of choice suggest themselves immediately:

(i)   Among putative authorities, choose the most up to date.

(ii) Among putative authorities, choose the ancients.

(iii) Among putative authorities, go by majority vote.

One might find maxim (i) appealing on the grounds that knowledge is cumulative and the latest authority is best able to correct the mistakes of earlier authorities. Maxim (ii) might be thought appealing on the grounds that the views of the ancients have, as we say, stood the test of time. Descartes does not deal explicitly here with maxim (i). Implicit reasoning I try to extract in a moment would, however, undermine it. As for maxim (ii), the trouble is obviously that putative authorities disagree among themselves. Descartes makes this objection forcefully in his earlier work, *Rules for the Direction of the Mind:* "But even if all [ancient] writers were sincere and open [an assumption Descartes has just vehemently rejected], and never tried to palm off doubtful matters as true, but instead put forward everything in good faith, we would always be uncertain which of them to believe, for hardly anything is said by one writer the contrary of which is not asserted by some other" (AT X, 367; CSM I, 13). That claim yields this argument:

(7)   For any ancient authority x and any subject y about which x makes pronouncements, x is to be believed about y if and only if there is no other ancient authority z such that x and z make contrary assertions about y.

(8)   For any ancient authority x and any subject y about which x makes pronouncements, there is always some other ancient authority z such that x and z make contrary assertions about y.

Therefore,

(9)   For any ancient authority x and any subject y about which x makes pronouncements, x is not to be believed about y.

Put simply,

(9′)   No ancient authority is to be believed about anything.

Descartes rejects maxim (iii) vehemently, both in the *Rules* and in the *Discourse*. In the latter work he says that "a majority vote is worthless as a proof of truths that are at all difficult to discover; for a single man is much more likely to hit upon them than a group of people" (AT VI, 16; CSM I, 119). The claim in the *Rules* is similar: "It would be of no use to count heads, so as to follow the view which many authorities hold. For if the question at issue is a difficult one, it is more likely that few, rather than many, should have been able to discover the truth about it" (AT X, 367; CSM I, 13).

There is a way of looking at the *Discourse,* however, that yields something more radical than what I call above the "argument for epistemic individualism." Surely Descartes does not really suppose that, had he had only one teacher, he *ought to have been* content to follow the opinions of that one teacher. Perhaps he has enough self-knowledge to realize that he *would* have been content to follow that one teacher's opinion. But once having lost that naivete and discovered that "nothing is too strange or incredible to have been said by some philosopher," Descartes has realized the futility of going by an expert's credentials alone.

Implicit in this section of the *Discourse,* then, is the following more radical argument for epistemic individualism:

(10) Either all the knowledge I can attain is to be found in myself and my own experience or else some knowledge is available to me from an outside expert.

(11) If some knowledge is available to me from an outside expert, then I can tell which experts are trustworthy independently of determining for myself whether what they have to say is true.

(12) I cannot tell which experts are trustworthy independently of determining for myself whether what they have to say is true.

Therefore,

(13) All the knowledge I can attain is to be found in myself and my own experience.

The conclusions of these two arguments for epistemic individualism ("I should become my own guide in seeking knowledge," and "All the knowledge I can attain is to be found in myself and my own experience") express serious ego isolation. The idea is that, when it comes to knowledge, I am simply on my own. No outside guide can relieve me of my responsibility; no outside authority can underwrite my knowledge claims for me.

As I have already indicated, Descartes himself seems to accept (13). Moreover, (10), (11), and (12) together give him a reason for accepting (13). But one who found (13) unacceptable could use this argument as a *reductio* to reject one or more of the premises. Premise (11) would be, perhaps, the most likely candidate for rejection. What makes (11) plausible is, I think, the notion that any knowledge I, in particular, have of some object *o* depends upon my having a blue-ribbon connection, a knowledge-making connection to *o* itself. That blue-ribbon connection might pass through a third party, some expert, say, as long as the part connecting me with the expert is also blue-ribbon. But if, by contrast, there were indeed experts with a blue-ribbon connection to *o*, but I had no blue-ribbon connection to them, that is, no foolproof way of deciding which one or ones to trust, and on which matters, then, even though *they* had knowledge, I could not share in it.

By contrast, someone who takes knowledge to be a social product, and not primarily, or at least not solely, a blue-ribbon connection between some individual knower and the object of knowledge, will insist that we often have to accept as our knowledge the opinion of experts whose competence we are incompetent to judge for ourselves. One virtue of the radical argument for a first-person perspective in philosophy, then, is that it helps us understand what distinguishes the philosopher who insists that it is solely individual knowers who have knowledge from the philosopher who thinks of knowledge as a social or institutional product.

That Descartes insists on what I have called the "blue-ribbon connection" for something to count as real knowledge is clear from various passages in his writings. Rules II and III of his *Rules for the Direction of the Mind* are especially helpful on this point. Consider this reasoning, to be found in the discussion of Rule III:

[E]ven if [the authorities] all agreed among themselves, their teaching would still not be all we need. For example, even though we know other people's demonstrations by heart, we shall never become mathematicians if we lack the intellectual aptitude to solve any given problem. And even though we have read all the arguments of Plato and Aristotle, we shall never become philosophers if we are unable to make a sound judgement on matters which come up for discussion; in this case what we would seem to have learnt would not be science [i.e., knowledge, *scientia*] but history. (AT X, 367; CSM I, 13)

A similar contrast between gaining real knowledge (*scientia*) and merely learning history, that is, learning what others have thought, is found in this passage from a letter of 8 February 1640 to Hogelande:

I am accustomed to distinguish two things in mathematics: history and knowledge [*scientia*]. By 'history' I understand everything that has already been discovered, and is contained in books. But by 'knowledge' I understand the skill to solve all questions and further to discover by one's own effort [*propria industria*] everything in this science that can be discovered by the human mind. Whoever has that skill is not much interested in other things [*aliena*] and can properly be called independent [*autarkés*]. And although one need not be totally ignorant of what is contained in books, a general knowledge of them suffices.[1]

---

1. Descartes, *Correspondance*, ed. Ch. Adam and G. Milhaud (Paris: Presses Universitaires de France, 1947), 4:31. This letter is not included in AT.

The idea here is pretty clearly that the independent investigator is the only one with true knowledge. Just as no one else can lead my own life for me, so no one else can gain my own knowledge for me. If I am to have knowledge, I must gain it for myself. The point in this passage is not the skeptical one of not knowing whom to believe, or on what basis. The point is rather that the attempt to acquire real knowledge by learning what others teach is doomed to failure. Having knowledge about x is different from knowing what even the most learned authorities say or think about x; the latter is only "history." "All knowledge," Descartes tells us at the beginning of his discussion of Rule II, "is certain and evident cognition [*omnis scientia est cognitio certa et evidens*]" (AT X, 362; CSM II, 10).

Along with Descartes's critique of the appeal to authority, there is in him a diminution of the role of the teacher. To be sure, Descartes sometimes presents his "do-it-yourself" approach to learning as simply an exuberant enthusiasm for figuring things out independently. He begins his discussion of Rule X this way:

> The natural bent of my mind, I confess, is such that the greatest pleasure I have taken in my studies has always come not from accepting the arguments of others but from discovering arguments by my own efforts. It was just this that attracted me to the study of the sciences while I was still in my youth. Whenever the title of a book gave promise of a new discovery, before I read any further I would try and see whether perhaps I could achieve a similar result by means of a certain innate discernment. And I took great care not to deprive myself of this innocent pleasure through a hasty reading of the book. (AT X, 403; CSM I, 35)

Yet something rather more interesting and philosophically more significant than the pursuit of harmless pleasure is suggested in other passages. Especially revealing is a letter to Beekman of 17 October 1630—at roughly the time Descartes was writing the *Rules,* but earlier than the *Discourse.* Descartes is discussing what one person can teach another. "Merely to repeat the views and maxims of philosophers," he writes, "is not to teach them." The first reason is that philosophers disagree among themselves. "Plato says one thing," Descartes continues, "Aristotle another, Epicurus another, Telesio, Campanella, Bruno, Basson, Vanini, and the innovators all say something different." Then comes this passage:

[I]f someone merely comes to believe something without being swayed by any authority or argument which he has learnt from others, this does not mean that he has been taught it by anyone, even though he may have heard many people say it. *It may even be that he really knows it, being impelled to believe it by true reasons, and that no one before him has ever known it, although they may have been of the same opinion because they deduced it from false principles.* (AT I, 158; K, 17; emphasis added)

It is pretty clear that really knowing something requires, according to Descartes's assumptions here, having what I have called a "blue-ribbon connection" to the thing known. And one may have that even though one's so-called teacher lacks it. Descartes adds this memorable comment: "If you know something, it is completely yours, even if you have learnt it from someone else" (AT I, 159; K, 17). This follows:

(14)   If the proposition that p is not completely mine, then I do not know that p.

And the reason I do not know what is not completely mine is that knowledge is "certain and evident cognition" (Rule II). If we are to gain knowledge of something, we must, each of us, individually and for ourselves, without reliance on any other person, possess it completely.

It is Descartes's thought about knowledge as a "do-it-yourself" achievement that leads him to his plan: to "reform [his] own thoughts and construct them upon a foundation

which is all [his] own" (*Discourse*, II; AT VI, 15; CSM I, 118).
This is the rational reconstruction of knowledge. Descartes
adopts for the first stages of his reconstruction of knowledge
the method of systematic doubt: to "reject as if absolutely false
everything in which I could imagine the least doubt, in order
to see if I was left believing anything that was entirely indubitable" (*Discourse*, IV; AT VI, 31–32, CSM I, 127).

᠗

Descartes's epistemic individualism can be identified as one
version of what is nowadays called "internalism" in epistemology. According to the version of internalism I have in
mind[2]—a version one finds, for example, in the writings of
Roderick Chisholm—"the things we know are justified for us
in the following sense: *we* can know what it is, on any occasion,
that constitutes our grounds, or reason, or evidence for thinking that we know."[3] As William P. Alston expresses roughly
the same idea, "whenever we are justified in a belief, we can
determine by reflection what it is that so justifies us."[4]

It bears mentioning that the embedded 'we' in Chisholm's
formulation is a 'we*' and the embedded 'us' in Alston's statement is an 'us*'. Thus, it is an implication of internalism so
understood that, if I know that *p*, then I can determine by
reflection what justifies me* in having the belief that *p* and
what constitutes the "grounds, or reason, or evidence for
thinking" that I* know that *p*. Statement (14) might reasonably be taken as an expression of this variety of internalism—
where an item of knowledge counts as being completely mine
just in case I can determine, by reflection, what justifies me*
in accepting it.

2. Versions of internalism are usefully surveyed in William P. Alston, "Internalism and Externalism in Epistemology," in his *Epistemic Justification: Essays in the Theory of Knowledge* (Ithaca, N.Y.: Cornell University Press, 1989).
3. *Theory of Knowledge* (Englewood Cliffs, N.J.: Prentice-Hall, 1966), 17.
4. *Epistemic Justification*, 212.

What makes internalism plausible—the idea of a "blue-ribbon connection" that I have been discussing in this chapter—also brings out part of the importance, for Descartes, of the rational reconstruction of knowledge. Once I have completed my reconstruction, I can confront each putative item of knowledge and determine whether I am justified in accepting it by testing it against my rational reconstruction of knowledge. Perhaps it will already be part of that reconstruction. Alternatively, it may belong to some justifiable extension of the reconstruction. If it is neither part of my already reconstructed knowledge nor a justifiable extension of that reconstruction, I am not justified in accepting it.

ॐ

Among commentators on Descartes, Bernard Williams is one of the few to ask why Descartes gives his project a first-person form, indeed, a first-person singular form. "It is an interesting and delicate question," writes Williams, ". . . at what point the first-personal bias, in any methodologically significant way, takes hold of Descartes's enquiry." Descartes introduces, Williams goes on,

> the search for truth in first-personal style in both the *Discourse* and the *Meditations* (the 'I' of the *Discourse* is more determinately the historical Descartes than is the soliloquizer of the *Meditations*), but this is not yet very heavily commital: the questions asked in the enquiry might, for all that, be of the form, 'what is true?' or even 'what is known?' On the other hand, Descartes certainly ends the Doubt in what he takes to be a radically first-personal situation, within the world of his own ideas, seeking a route to a world outside that. Is there anything in his process of enquiry itself which determines the transition?[5]

Williams then asks whether Descartes's search for truth might as well be expressed in the first-person plural. "Might it not,"

5. *Descartes*, 68.

he asks, "be a collective enterprise? For Descartes, certainly it is not; even if he conducts enquiry as our representative, he does it by himself. But perhaps this is not necessary. . . . it is entirely natural to take 'our' representations to be collective representations, social products, shared by individuals in a society or cultural group."[6]

It is only fair to note that in this passage Williams is not doing pure scholarship on Descartes. Instead, he is asking whether what he calls the "project of pure enquiry", which he takes Descartes to be pursuing in both the *Discourse* and the *Meditations,* could as well be thought of as a collective enterprise. "An obvious reply to such suggestions," he goes on, "is that a group's knowledge or belief cannot be ultimate or irreducible—it must ultimately be individuals who are in such states, and to speak of the knowledge of a group, or of a society's representation of reality, must involve some kind of fiction."[7]

Williams does, then, offer a response on behalf of collective inquiry. But without examining that response, we can say, I think, that the individualist's position ("it must ultimately be individuals who are in such states") is Descartes's own. If the "project of pure enquiry" does not have the singular first-personalization of knowledge built into it, then it fails to represent fully Descartes's own project.

That the first-personalization of knowledge in Descartes is what leads to the method of doubt can already be seen in Rule II, in these, the first four sentences of discussion:

> All knowledge is certain and evident cognition. Someone who has doubts about many things is no wiser than one who has never given them a thought; indeed, he appears less wise if he has formed a false opinion about any of them. Hence it is better never to study at all than to occupy ourselves with objects which are so difficult that we are unable to distinguish what is true

6. Ibid., 70.
7. Ibid.

from what is false, and are forced to take the doubtful as certain; for in such matters the risk of diminishing our knowledge is greater than our hope of increasing it. So, in accordance with this Rule, we reject all such merely probable cognition and resolve to believe only what is perfectly known and incapable of being doubted. (AT X, 362; CSM I, 10)

If, in accord with Williams's suggestion, some community were to search for truth as a collective inquiry, either that inquiry would result in certain and evident cognition in some of the individuals who made up the group or it would not. If it did, that certain and evident cognition would be, in Descartes's view, the sum of the knowledge the collective effort produced. If it did not, there would be, in his view, no knowledge at all produced by the inquiry. In either case, the result on this score would be Descartes's measure of the inquiry's success. What Williams refers to as a "bias" for the first-person singular in Descartes lies at the very heart of Descartes's internalist enterprise.

∂❧

Descartes presents his search for truth in autobiographical form—fairly straightforwardly in the *Discourse* and through the stylized form of first-person reflections in the *Meditations*. Is that search itself guided by an 'I*' question?

"[U]nable to choose anyone whose opinions struck me as preferable to those of all others," Descartes writes in Part II of the *Discourse*, "I found myself as it were forced to become my own guide" (AT VI, 16; CSM I, 119). So his question is 'Who should be my guide?' But guide in the search for what?

In the next paragraph Descartes speaks of "seeking the true method of attaining the knowledge of everything within [his] mental capabilities." And in Part III he speaks of "following a path by which I thought I was sure to acquire all the knowledge of which I was capable . . ." (AT VI, 28; CSM I,

125). So it seems that the guide is to help in the search for knowledge within his capabilities or in the search for all he can know. Descartes's overall question, then, is this:

(15) Who should guide me in the search for all that I* can know?

His answer to (15) is, of course, the internalist reply: 'I should guide myself.' For Descartes, guiding himself in the search for all that he* can know eventually leads him (i) to establish that he* exists; (ii) to prove that he* is a thinking thing; (iii) to consider how he* knows whether he* is then dreaming; and (iv) to ask how he knows that not all life is a dream he* is having.

Early on in Meditation III Descartes writes, "I am certain that I am a thinking thing. Do I now therefore also know what is required for my being certain about anything?" (AT VII, 34; CSM II, 24). The question here is this:

(16) Do I know what is required for it to be the case that I* am certain that p?

This question lies at the heart of Descartes's internalism. Unless he can answer (16) affirmatively, he will not be able, he thinks, to determine by reflection whether he is justified in holding any given belief.

Descartes's response to (16) is to say that I can be certain that p if and only if my idea that p is clear and distinct. Clarity and distinctness, he supposes, guarantee truth and show that one is justified in accepting whatever idea has that feature.

Later on in Meditation II, Descartes comments, "I must consider whether there is anything in the idea [of God] which could not have originated in myself" (AT VI, 45; CSM II, 31). Two paragraphs later is this question: "For how could I understand that I doubted or desired—that is, lacked something—and that I was not wholly perfect, unless there were in me some idea of a more perfect being which enabled me to recognize my own defects by comparison?" (AT VI, 46; CSM II, 31). Part of the question here is this:

(17)   Could I understand that I* am not wholly perfect if I did not have some idea of a more perfect being?

This question is part of one of Descartes's efforts to prove the existence of God.

The list of significant 'I*' questions in the *Meditations* could be continued. In fact, it would hardly be an exaggeration to say that it is largely 'I*' questions that structure Descartes's rational reconstruction of knowledge as it is presented in the *Meditations* and the *Discourse*.[8] Once one appreciates Des-

8. Here and elsewhere in this work I have concentrated especially on the *Meditations* for my interpretations of Descartes. I have also paid significant attention to the *Discourse*, but I have tended to ignore the *Principles*, which is the third main statement of Descartes's philosophy. Occasionally the *Principles* is also clearly I*-driven, as in this passage: "For it is a contradiction to suppose that what thinks does not, at the very time when it is thinking, exist. Accordingly, this piece of knowledge—*I* [*think*], *therefore I exist*—is the first and most certain of all to occur to anyone who philosophizes in an orderly way" (AT VIIIA, 7; CSM II, 195). Quite clearly Descartes's claim here answers the 'I*' question, 'Can I be certain that I* exist?' In the very next paragraph of the *Principles*, Descartes reverts to the first-person plural. The question he tries to answer there, I should say, is a 'we*' question: "For if we, who are supposing that everything which is distinct from us is false [i.e., counterfeit], examine what we are, we see very clearly that neither extension nor shape nor local motion, nor anything of this kind which is attributable to a body, belongs to our nature, but that thought alone belongs to it." Here Descartes's question seems to be roughly this: 'What can we, who suppose that nothing besides us* really is what it seems to be, see belongs to the nature we* have?' Answer: 'Thought alone.' Descartes, I should say, intends for his readers, individually, to ask this question of themselves: 'Supposing that nothing besides me is what it appears to be, what can I see belongs to the nature I* have?'

In my view, then, 'I*' questions also drive much of the reasoning in the *Principles*, though this fact is certainly less obvious than is the analogous fact about the *Meditations* and the *Discourse*. Indeed, I do not think it would ever have occurred to me that there was an 'I*' question underlying the second *Principles* passage above if I had not first seen the clear parallel between it and Meditation II: "But what shall I now say that I[*] am, when I am supposing

cartes's internalism, this makes perfect sense. For internalism is the view that I must be able to tell, on reflection, whether I* am justified in holding this or that belief. And Cartesian internalism is the view that I can do this by reference to a rational reconstruction of knowledge put together from my* own point of view.

It may come as a surprise to the reader to learn that Augustine, in contrast to Descartes, is not an internalist in the Cartesian sense under discussion. That he is not should become clear in the next chapter. Once one has appreciated that Augustine is not an internalist in epistemology, it becomes clearer why 'I*' questions play a more limited role in his thought than they do in Descartes's.

---

that there is some supremely powerful and, if it is permissible to say so, malicious deceiver, who is deliberately trying to trick me[*] in every way he can?" (AT VII, 26; CSM II, 18).

[11]

Augustine on
Outside Authority

In some of his earliest works, such as the *Soliloquies*, Augustine frames a project of rational inquiry that resembles, in various limited but nontrivial respects, Descartes's rational reconstruction of knowledge. Just as Descartes announces his topic for the *Meditations* as "God and the soul" and his intent to provide "demonstrative proofs" (AT VII, 1; CSM II, 3), so there is this exchange between Augustine and Reason near the beginning of the *Soliloquies:*

> REASON: What then do you wish to know?
> AUGUSTINE: All that I have mentioned in my prayer.
> REASON: Briefly summarize it.
> AUGUSTINE: I desire to know God and the soul.
> REASON: Nothing more?
> AUGUSTINE: Nothing whatever.
> REASON: Begin your quest then.
>
> *(Soliloquies* I.2.7)

No philosophical inquiry of Augustine's is, however, as broad or as thorough as that which leads Descartes to the rational reconstruction of knowledge in the *Discourse* and *Meditations*. And none is like Descartes's in being conducted from the standpoint of thought's ego. Furthermore, none calls into question, as part of the inquiry, the very existence of "the external world," as happens in Descartes. It is this last feature that most firmly establishes the centrality of thought's ego in Descartes's philosophy. Inquiry in Augustine is conducted from the standpoint of faith. In fact, the passage above is preceded by a prayer *to* God. Nothing like that is to be found in Descartes, certainly not before the existence of God is even proved.

In Book II of *On Free Choice of the Will*, Augustine says to Evodius, "At any rate you are quite certain that God exists." Evodius replies, "I firmly believe it, but I do not know it." There follows a discussion of "belief in search of understanding," a section of which ends with Evodius's saying, "But we want to know and to understand what we believe" (II.2.5).

As we have noted, Descartes's method of systematic or hyperbolical doubt requires him to "reject as if absolutely false everything in which [he] could imagine the least doubt" (*Discourse*, IV; AT VI, 31; CSM I, 127). By contrast, Augustine takes at least some of what he believes as an unproved basis for thought and action and then seeks to find reasons for what he believes, so that he can understand it properly. The standpoint of faith Augustine adopts throughout his writing carries with it, as we might expect, a very different attitude toward authority than what we find in Descartes. It is the project of this chapter to bring out some of Augustine's ideas on authority and how those ideas bear on the place of thought's ego in his philosophy.

≈&

In the previous chapter I characterized Descartes's internalism as a rejection, on philosophical grounds, of the appeal to outside authority. In resolving to be his own guide in the search for what he can know, Descartes in effect resolves to make himself his own authority. Augustine, by contrast, never expresses any such ambition. Even in his most rational and systematic moods, Augustine never tries to undermine all appeal to outside authority.[1]

Consider Augustine's *Confessions*. That work is his spiritual autobiography, but it is also his intellectual autobiography and, in that respect, it is like Descartes's *Discourse*. But, whereas in Part II of the *Discourse* Descartes brings out an epistemological problem about the appeal to outside authority, Augustine writes this:

> From now on I began to prefer the Catholic teaching. The Church demanded that certain things should be believed even though they could not be proved, for if they could be proved, not all men could understand the proof, and some could not be proved at all. I thought the Church was entirely honest in this and far less pretentious than the Manichees, who laughed at people who took things on faith, and made rash promises of scientific knowledge, and then put forward a whole system of preposterous inventions which they expected their followers to believe on trust because they could not be proved. (*Confessions* 6.5)

We are not given, immediately, any indication of the range of things that, as it turns out, should be believed though they "could not be proved at all." But soon there is a suggestion that their number and variety is rather large indeed. In the very next paragraph Augustine writes this: "And so, since we are too weak to discover the truth by reason alone and for this reason need the authority of sacred books, I began to believe that you would never have invested the Bible with such con-

---

1. Kurt Flasch, in his *Augustin: Einführung in sein Denken* (Stuttgart: Reclam, 1980), 83, claims that Augustine first supposes authority to be a "placeholder for reason" but later comes to give it a more independent role. Although there is certainly some basis for his claim, I see the attitude of late Augustine as much more like that of middle, and even early, Augustine than does Flasch. After all, even in *On True Religion*, a work of the early middle period, Augustine supposes that the most reason can do for some truths accepted on authority is to show them to have been "possible and fitting."

spicuous authority in every land unless you had intended it to be the means by which we should look for you and believe in you" (*Confessions*, VI.5).

We know from various of Augustine's writings that he supposes all of the Bible—not just, as the Manicheans thought, the New Testament, but the Old Testament as well—to be invested with divine authority. That being so, the scope of things that cannot be proved at all is large indeed. Let us call the things, whatever they are, that should be believed, even though they cannot be proved, "credibilia." It is Augustine's view that credibilia should be accepted from an authority—whether it be the the church, the Bible, or perhaps some secular authority.

How might one seek to justify such a position?

First of all, there is the moral argument. One of Augustine's favorite examples of a credibile is the proposition that so and so are one's parents—in Augustine's own case the proposition that Monica and Patricius are his own mother and father. Here is one of several passages in which Augustine discusses this kind of case:

Now I ask, if nothing which is not known is to be believed, how will children serve their parents and love them with mutual dutifulness if they do not believe that they are their parents. That cannot be known by reason. Who the father is is believed on the authority of the mother, and as to the mother, midwives, nurses, slaves have to be believed, for the mother can deceive, being herself deceived by having her son stolen and another put in his place. But we believe, and that without any hesitation, what we confess we do not know. Otherwise who does not see the dutifulness, the most sacred bond of the human race, might be violated by the most overbearing wickedness? Who would be so mad as to think him blameworthy who performed the duties due to those whom he believed to be his parents even if they were not his parents in reality? Who, on the other hand, would not think him worthy of banishment who did not love those who were probably his true parents on the ground that he feared he might love those who were not his parents. I could bring many instances to show that nothing would remain stable in human society if we determined to believe nothing that we could not scientifically establish. (*The Usefulness of Belief*, 12.26)

Augustine's idea is that, for some credibilia, it would be morally wrong to reject the claims of the relevant authorities. Claims about one's immediate parentage are such credibilia. Other things being equal, one is justified in believing Mother's claim to be one's mother and Father's claim to be one's father just because, in the absence of special reasons to doubt these claims, it would be morally wrong to doubt their authority on this question.

Augustine's main argument for accepting certain credibilia on the basis of authority is, however, rather different from this moral argument. It rests on a claim that some things cannot even be understood unless they are first believed. Here Augustine gives it on his own behalf in his dialogue with Evodius near the beginning of Book II of *On Free Choice of the Will:* "You remember the position we adopted at the beginning of our former discussion. We cannot deny that believing and knowing are different things, and that in matters of great importance, pertaining to divinity, we must first believe before we seek to know. Otherwise the words of the prophet would be vain, where he says: 'Except ye believe ye shall not understand'" (Isaiah 7:9 LXX) (II.2.6).[2] This Augustinian idea finds a famous echo in St. Anselm's *Proslogion*. In Chapter 1 of that work, just before he offers the ontological argument, Anselm writes this: "For I do not seek to understand that I may believe, but I believe in order to understand. For

2. Norman Kretzmann points out in a footnote to his helpful article "Faith Seeks, Understanding Finds," in *Christian Philosophy*, ed. Thomas P. Flint (Notre Dame, Ind.: University of Notre Dame Press, 1990), 1–36, that Augustine's Latin version of the verse from Isaiah is a mistranslation. The modern Revised Standard Version gives this verse as, "If you will not believe, surely you shall not be established."

this also I believe—that unless I believed, I should not understand."[3]

It is well to note Augustine's restriction in the quotation from *On Free Choice of the Will* "in matters of great importance, pertaining to divinity." It is such matters about which Augustine says that "we must first believe before we seek to know." Augustine is not committed to supposing this about all objects of knowledge.

There is certainly a strong strain of Platonism in Augustine according to which a significant range of a priori truths can be known directly by the intellect without appeal to outside authority. In his *Confessions* he says this about "the innumerable principles and laws of numbers and dimensions": "We know them simply by recognizing them inside ourselves without reference to any material object" (X.12). Yet a caveat must be added to this caveat. Although Augustine seems, even in later life, to maintain the view that important truths of reason can be known without any appeal whatsoever to outside authority, he seems to become gradually less confident about how extensive and reliable these powers of independent reason are (see, e.g., *City of God*, XI.2, which we discuss in Chapter 13). It is not that he comes to think that reason may give us the wrong answer in, say, mathematics; it is rather that reason may just "black out" (see *The Literal Meaning of Genesis*, XII.14.29). Even more important, he comes in later life to view what is available to reason alone as much less important than those "great and hidden truths" that must be believed, indeed, believed on authority, before they can be understood.

ào

Are there reasonable constraints on whom or what we may accept as authoritative? Clearly Augustine thinks so. We may

3. St. Anselm, *Basic Writings*, trans. S. N. Deane (La Salle, Ill.: Open Court, 1961), 7.

divide them into prior constraints and subsequent constraints.

We can begin with prior constraints. "We must have recourse, then," Augustine writes in *The Catholic Way of Life*, "to the teachings of those who were in all probability wise. This is as far as reason can take us" (7.11). Augustine must think that we can make some preliminary judgments about who is "in all probability wise." We can expect, with some probability, that these teachers will not only function as good authorities themselves but will lead us to other good authorities, for example, to the Bible.

What marks off a teacher who is "in all probability wise" and distinguishes that teacher from others less likely to be wise? Augustine looks for such traits of character as openness and consistency. Thus he never tires of complaining that the Manicheans "laughed at people who took things on faith, and made rash promises of scientific knowledge, and then put forward a whole system of preposterous inventions which they expected their followers to believe on trust because they could not be proved" (*Confessions*, VI.5). So Augustine rejected the Manicheans as teachers, not just, or perhaps even primarily, on the basis of an assessment of what doctrines they taught, but on the basis of their inconsistency and deceit.

What, now, about subsequent constraints on who should serve as an authority? In his *Confessions*, Augustine gives us several examples of cases in which he thinks he can *dis*prove a doctrine that either he or someone else has accepted from an authority. He tells about discrediting astrologers by appeal to cases of simultaneous births, in which the fortunes of one child are vastly preferable to those of the other. In one case the son of a slave was born at the exact same time, he writes, as the son of a wealthy nobleman. Thus,

> the slave was born under the very same constellations, and if he had asked me to tell him [the meaning of the stars under which he was born], my interpretation of them could not have been

true unless I saw in them a family of the meanest sort, the status of a slave, and various other details entirely different from and inconsistent with those which applied to [the wealthy freeman's son,] Firminus. This proved that if I were to say what was actually the truth, I should give a different answer to each, though the stars I read were the same; whereas, if I gave the same answer to each, I would be wrong in fact. (*Confessions*, VII.6)

We need not, according to Augustine, examine further the character of a given astrologer, or the accuracy of a given prediction; cases of simultaneous births, where the children have vastly different fortunes, show that astrologers cannot be credible authorities on the fortunes and misfortunes that await us.

Here is another kind of case. The Manicheans claim that, "because they have observed that there are two wills at odds with each other when we try to reach a decision, we must therefore have two minds of different natures, one good, the other evil" (*Confessions* VIII.10). Augustine seems to understand the operative principle to be something like this:

(1)   If *x* wants to do *a* and *x* also wants to do *b* and *x* believes that doing *a* is incompatible with doing *b*, then either doing *a* is an expression of *x*'s good mind and doing *b* an expression of *x*'s evil mind, or vice versa.

But (1), he thinks, is clearly unacceptable, as this reasoning shows:

If there were as many different natures in us as there are conflicting wills, we should have a great many more natures than merely two. Suppose that someone is trying to decide whether to go to the theatre or to the Manichees' meeting-house. The Manichees will say, "Clearly he has two natures, the good one bringing him here to us and the bad one leading him away." . . . [But suppose] then that one of us is wavering between two con-

flicting wills and cannot make up his mind whether to go to the
theatre or to our church. Will not the Manichees be embar-
rassed to know what to say? Either they must admit—which
they will not do—that it is a good will which brings a man to our
church, just as in their opinion it is a good will which brings
their own communicants and adherents to their church; or they
must presume that there are two evil natures and two evil minds
in conflict in one man. If they think this, they will disprove their
own theory that there is one good and one evil will in man.
(*Confessions*, VII:10)

Beyond the question of prior and subsequent constraints
on whom one should appeal to as an authority, does Augustine think there can be positive considerations that favor
one authority over another? I think it is clear that he does. In
his *The Usefulness of Belief* he says that the authority of the
Catholic church is made appealing "partly by miracles, and
partly by the multitudes of its adherents" (16.34). Earlier on
he says that he has come to believe in Christ "on the ground of
a report confirmed by its ubiquity, by its antiquity, and by the
general consent of mankind" (14.31). And in the *Confessions*
he says to God, "I began to believe that you would never have
invested the Bible with such conspicuous authority in every
land unless you had intended it to be the means by which we
should look for you and believe in you" (VI.5). But he never
offers a systematic account of the grounds on which one authority is preferable to another.

There is another consideration. Augustine obviously has
the idea of faith as a virtue. It is important to him to mark off
faith from credulity, which he does with some care in *The
Usefulness of Belief*, 9.22. No doubt the prior and subsequent
constraints on appropriate appeals to authority go some way
toward distinguishing the person of faith from the merely
credulous person. But perhaps there is a useful interplay between thinking about appropriate constraints on the appeal to
authority and thinking about the kinds of people who insist
on them or ignore them.

ટ**

Given his acceptance of "outside" authority, Augustine is never driven to thought's ego as an epistemological stronghold. Although in his *Soliloquies* he certainly does reason in the epistemological privacy of a dialogue with Reason rather systematically through what he considers himself to believe, he has no philosophical ground for preferring that mode of discourse to the dialogue with Evodius in *On Free Choice of the Will*, where he also reasons systematically through some of what he believes. Although a version of the cogito appears in that dialogue, it too appears in a conversational exchange:

> AUGUSTINE: First, then, to begin with what is most obvious, I ask you: "Do you exist?" Are you perhaps afraid to be deceived by that question? But if you did not exist it would be impossible for you to be deceived.
> EVODIUS: Proceed to your other questions.
>
> (II.3.7)

There is here no effort to structure the inquiry as a whole from the point of view of thought's ego. How could there be, since it is put in dialogue form? No question arises about the existence of the "external world" or the existence of other minds. Augustine and his interlocutor seek together, drawing on outside authority, to "learn to know" (II.2.6) what they already believe. No effort is made to shake or winnow those beliefs, in the manner of Descartes. "This is the course prescribed by the prophet who says: 'Unless you believe, you shall not understand'" (*On Free Choice of the Will*, I.2.4).

[12]

Augustine on
the Teacher Within

Little by little I began to realize where I was and to want to make my wishes known to others, who might satisfy them. But this I could not do, because my wishes were inside me, while other people were outside, and they had no faculty which could penetrate my mind. So I would toss my arms and legs about and make noises, hoping that such few sighs as I could make would show my meaning, though they were quite unlike what they were meant to mime. And if my wishes were not carried out, either because they had not been understood or because what I wanted would have harmed me, I would get cross with my elders, who were not at my beck and call, and with people who were not my servants, simply because they did not attend to my wishes; and I would take my revenge by bursting into tears. (*Confessions*, I.6)

In this passage Augustine portrays himself as a baby before he had learned his first conventional language. As he depicts himself here, he is a creature with wishes who wants to express those wishes to others. He is capable of making a few signs that are meant to mime his desires, or perhaps the objects of his desires, though they, as Augustine admits, fail to resemble what they were meant to mime. Finally, he is capable of taking revenge on those who are unresponsive to his entreaties.

As Augustine pictures his baby self, then, he certainly has desires, thoughts about how to satisfy those desires, and even thoughts about how to punish those who fail to help him satisfy his desires. But he is incapable of expressing his desires adequately or of asking others for help in satisfying them. So here is clearly a picture of significant ego isolation.

It is important to see, though, that the ego isolation portrayed in this passage is not brought on by what, after Descartes, has come to be called "the problem of the external world." Augustine does not portray his baby self as concerned about whether those images before him are the appearances of solid and independently existing objects. As we concluded in Chapter 6, Augustine never thinks of himself as a subject for which the existence of all bodies might be philosophically problematic. Nor does he, as if anticipating Descartes, portray his baby self as being bewildered by the array of conflicting truths his elders wish to foist off on him and, for that reason, trying to reconstruct for himself what, if anything, he can legitimately claim to know. Rather, his concern is the meanings of words. He is like the sole survivor of a destroyed civilization who, having been captured by an alien enemy, finds that he cannot understand the language of his captors. He can talk and reason with himself in his native language (in the case of baby Augustine the language must have been "Mentalese"), but he is utterly bewildered by what people in the society around him are saying.

Later in the *Confessions*, in a passage Wittgenstein has made famous, Augustine gives this account of how he tried to break out of that semantic isolation:

> It was not my elders who showed me the words by some set system of instruction, in the way that they taught me to read long afterwards; but, instead, I taught myself by using the intelligence which you, my God, gave to me. For when I tried to express my meaning by crying out and making various sounds and movements, so that my wishes should be obeyed, I found

that I could not convey all that I meant or make myself under-stood by everyone whom I wish to understand me. So my memory prompted me. I noticed that people would name some object and then turn towards whatever it was they had named. I watched them and understood that the sound they made when they wanted to indicate that particular thing was the name which they gave to it, and their actions clearly showed what they meant, for there is a kind of universal language, consisting of expressions of the face and eyes, gestures and tones of voice, which can show whether a person means to ask for something and get it, or refuse it and have nothing to do with it. So by hearing words arranged in various phrases and constantly repeated, I gradually pieced together what they stood for, and when my tongue had mastered the pronunciation, I began to express my wishes by means of them. In this way I made my wants known to my family and they made theirs known to me. (I.8.)

As Augustine tells things in this passage, language acquisition for him was a complete success story. But if we look at the most interesting work of his devoted solely to the philosophy of language, the early dialogue *Concerning the Teacher,* a somewhat different story emerges.[1] This passage from that dialogue is especially important:

AUGUSTINE: Come now, tell me, if I, knowing absolutely nothing of the meaning of the word ['walking'] should ask you while you are in the act of walking what walking is, how would you teach me?

ADEODATUS [Augustine's son and, in this dialogue, his interlocutor]: I should walk somewhat more quickly in order that

1. The other work devoted to language is *De dialectica.* But Augustine also has interesting things to say about language in his *Christian Instruction (De doctrina christiana)* and *The Trinity.* For something of the broader picture, see R. A. Markus, "St. Augustine on Signs," and B. Darrell Jackson, "The Theory of Signs in St. Augustine's *De Doctrina Christiana,*" in *Augustine: A Collection of Critical Essays,* ed. R. A. Markus (Garden City: Anchor, 1972), as well as Christopher Kirwan, *Augustine* (London: Routledge, 1989), 35–59.

after your question your attention might be directed to something new. And yet I should do only what was to be shown.
AUGUSTINE: Do you not know that walking is one thing and
hurrying another? For he who walks need not immediately
hurry, and he who hurries does not necessarily walk, since we
speak of hurrying in writing and reading and in innumerable
other things. Hence, if after my question you were to do
more quickly what you were doing already, I should think
walking to be merely hurrying.

(3.6)

Although Augustine does not actually state any general principle of ambiguity in this dialogue, his discussion suggests that
he would subscribe to the following principle of the ambiguity
of ostension:

(1)   For any general term T whose meaning m can be
      given in ostension and for any concrete attempt to
      give the meaning of T in ostension, there is some
      different meaning m' such that, to judge by this
      attempt at ostension, one could as reasonably conclude
      that T has meaning m' as meaning m.

On the face of it, the account of successful language acquisition in Book I of the *Confessions* is at odds with this principle.
If there is no such thing as a thoroughly unequivocal ostension, how could the actions of speakers around baby Augustine ever get him to understand "that the sound they made
when they wanted to indicate that particular thing was the
name they gave it"?

In *Concerning the Teacher*, Augustine gives two answers,
which he seems to consider equivalent. One is that the learner
who is intelligent enough finally catches on to what is being
ostended. The other is that Christ, the teacher "within," and
only that inner teacher, can make clear what the word means.
Here is a crucial passage from the dialogue that makes his
point the first way:

AUGUSTINE: For consider, if someone unskilled in the art of bird-catching, which is done with reeds and bird-lime, should happen upon a fowler, carrying his instruments as he walked along, though not fowling at the time, he would hasten to follow and in wonderment he would reflect and ask himself, as indeed he might, what the man's equipment meant. Now if the fowler, seeing himself watched, were to exhibit his art, and skilfully employ the reed, and then noting a little bird nearby, if he were to charm, approach, and capture it with his reed and hawk, would the fowler not teach his observer without the use of signification, but rather by means of the thing itself which the observer desired to know?

ADEODATUS: I fear this observer of bird-catching is like the man whom I referred to above, who inquires about walking; for it does not seem that in this case the entire art of fowling is exhibited.

AUGUSTINE: It is easy to free you from that worry. For I suggest that an observer might be intelligent enough to recognize the whole complexity of the art from what he saw. It is enough for our purposes if certain men can be taught without signs about some things, if indeed not about all things.

ADEODATUS: To that I can add that if the learner be very intelligent he will know what walking is fully when it has been shown by a few steps.

AUGUSTINE: That is agreeable. And I not only do not object, but I approve of your statement.

(10.32)

This story fits well with the comment at the beginning of the second *Confessions* passage above, including this statement: "It was not my elders who showed me [the meaning of] the words . . . but, instead, I taught myself by using the intelligence which you, my God, gave to me."

Here is an example of Augustine putting his point in the second way:

Concerning universals of which we can have knowledge, we do not listen to anyone speaking and making sounds outside our-

selves. We listen to Truth which presides over our minds within
us, though of course we may be bidden to listen by someone
using words. Our real Teacher is he who is so listened to, who is
said to dwell in the inner man, namely Christ, that is, the un-
changeable power and eternal wisdom of God. To this wisdom
every rational soul gives heed. . . . (*Concerning the Teacher*,
11.38)[2]

Augustine's position in *Concerning the Teacher* seems to be
this. We learn the meaning of some words by having them
explained in terms of other words. But to connect our language with the empirical world, some of our words, it seems,
must be learned through ostension. Even when we learn what
a word means through ostension, however, it is not really the
ostender who teaches us what the word means but rather the
teacher "within." The teacher "outside" may provide a learning context and even a stimulus to learn. But, at least in part
because of the ambiguity of ostension, each of us has to figure
out for ourselves the meaning of the word ostended.[3] Equiv-
alently, it is the "teacher within" who teaches us what the word
means. Here then is an important line of reasoning in Augustine, which we might call the "argument for semantic individualism":

(2)   Either I have to figure out for myself, learning only
       from the teacher within, how language connects with
       the world, or else there are occasions on which a
       teacher outside can make the connection between
       language and the world for me by unambiguously
       ostending the meaning of a word.

2. From the translation by John H. S. Burleigh, *Augustine: Earlier Writings*,
in *The Library of Christian Classics*, vol. 6 (Philadelphia: Westminster Press,
1953), 95.
3. The reasoning in the dialogue is much more complex than I have indicated here. But the point about the ambiguity of ostension is sufficient for
our purposes.

(3)   There are no occasions on which a teacher outside can make the connection between language and the world for me by unambiguously ostending the meaning of a word.

Therefore,

(4)   I have to figure out entirely for myself, learning only from the teacher within, how language connects with the world.

In formulating this argument I have contented myself with the rather vague formulation "how language connects with the world." On a basic level, what is at stake is the meaning of words. But, Augustine moves back and forth quite easily between questions about, say, what the word 'walking' means and questions about what walking is. So figuring out how language connects with the world is also, for him, figuring out what the world is itself like. What this argument brings out is, I think, a kind of semantic ego isolation. One might have thought that learning a language was a question of taking over from other people a knowledge, or capacity, that they already have. Learning would be "by transfer." Augustine's reasoning is meant to convince us that this is not so, that we are, each of us, individually, on our own. We are not, of course, completely on our own, since there is the teacher "within." But crucial help is lacking from other language users "outside."

There is thus an important difference between Augustine's views on language learning and his views on the learning of nonlinguistic truths. For language learning one must rely, he thinks, on the teacher within. But there is no indication that he thinks this about learning in general. And when it comes to certain nonlinguistic truths, especially the divine truths, he insists that one must rely on outside teachers and even on outside authorities. How these two views about learning fit together perhaps becomes clearer as we go along.

❧

Augustine's philosophical interest in language continues throughout his life. One thing we see in the development of his thought, from the time he wrote *Concerning the Teacher* in 389 until he wrote the *Confessions* over a decade later, is a tendency to become more and more preoccupied with philosophically problematic terms. 'Walking' and 'bird-catching' are not, for him, philosophically problematic terms. 'God' is. So are 'time', 'evil', 'memory', and 'creation'—to mention some of his most obvious preoccupations in the *Confessions*. For the rest of his life Augustine struggles with these terms and with the concepts they express. Throughout his life he remains dissatisfied with what he can say about them.

It is worthwhile at this point making another comparison with Descartes. In Meditation III Descartes tells us that "the idea I have of God [is] the truest and most clear and distinct of all my ideas" (AT VII, 46; CSM II, 32). And in the Reply to Objections II he makes this instructive remark:

> No one can possibly go wrong when he tries to form a correct conception of the idea of God, provided he is willing to attend to the nature of a supremely perfect being. But some people muddle things up by including other attributes, which leads them to speak in a contradictory way: they construct an imaginary idea of God, and then—quite reasonably—go on to say that the God who is represented by this muddled idea does not exist. (AT VII, 138; CSM II, 99)

Augustine, by contrast, finds the idea of God endlessly problematic. In his *Confessions* he recounts his difficulty in thinking of God, or anything else, as a spiritual substance. His problem was to conceive a spiritual substance. At one point he says he "could form not the vaguest idea, even with the help of allegory, of how there could be a substance that was spiritual . . ." (VI.3). At a later point he admits that "although I did not imagine you [any longer] in the shape of a human body, I could not free myself from the thought that you were some kind of bodily substance extended in space, either permeating the world or diffused in infinity beyond it" (VII.1). Still later, he reports further success: "Though I was thwarted by my wish to know more, I was conscious of what it was that my mind was too clouded to see. I was certain both that you are and that you are infinite, though without extent in terms of space either limited or unlimited" (VII.20).

To these difficulties of conceiving a spiritual substance must be added the formidable problems of conceiving the Trinity. Consider this passage from *Christian Instruction* (*De doctrina christiana*):

> It is not easy to find a term which appropriately defines such great excellence, unless it is better to say that this Trinity is one God from whom, through whom, and in whom all things exist. Thus, there are Father, Son, and Holy Ghost. Each of these individually is God. At the same time They are all one God. Each of Them individually comprises the fullness of divine substance. At the same time They are all only one Substance. The Father is neither the Son nor the Holy Ghost; the Son is neither the Father nor the Holy Ghost; the Holy Ghost is neither the Father nor the Son. The Father is only the Father; the Son, only the Son; The Holy Ghost, only the Holy Ghost. . . .

> Have I spoken or given utterance to anything worthy of God? On the contrary, I realize that I have done nothing but wish to speak. But, if I have spoken anything, it is not what I wanted to say. How am I aware of this, unless God is ineffable? [Yet] what I have said would not have been said, if [God] had been ineffable. For this reason God should not be spoken of even as ineffable, because, when we say this word, we are saying something about Him. There is some contradiction of terms, since, if that is

ineffable which cannot be spoken of, a thing is not ineffable
which can be called ineffable. (I.5–6)

Augustine's worry that we cannot correctly say of God even
that he is ineffable (because describing him in that way would
be describing him and thus revealing that the description is
false) is characteristic; in fact, it is both characteristic of Augustine's thought in general and also characteristic of his
thoughts about God and the term 'God' (*deus*) in particular. It
contrasts clearly and instructively with Descartes's confident
assurance, "No one can possibly go wrong when he tries to
form a correct conception of the idea of God, provided he is
willing to attend to the nature of a supremely perfect being"
(AT VII, 138; CSM II, 99).

To be sure, Descartes does suppose that it may be at least a
preliminary task of philosophy to standardize the use of
words. Thus he has a discussion under Rule XIII of his *Rules
for the Direction of the Mind* on difficulties that arise from "the
obscurity of the language employed." But it turns out that all
he has in mind is sloppiness in the use of language. That
sloppiness can be eliminated, he supposes, by taking more
care and by simply agreeing among ourselves how to use
words. Indeed, "if philosophers always agreed about the
meaning of words," he adds optimistically, "their controver-
sies would almost all be at an end" (AT X, 434; CSM I, 54).
There is no hint, here or elsewhere in Descartes, that the
meaning of the most philosophically interesting words may be
deeply problematic.

ઝ⊾

One response to the problem posed by the principle of the
ambiguity of ostension is to say that language is, after all, a
social, or institutional, phenomenon. When we learn a language, it is not that we connect words to the appropriate
things in the world; rather, we learn socially acceptable ways

of behaving linguistically. If we develop the ability to use words like 'wall' or 'bird-catching' in socially acceptable ways, we have acquired those words. We have learned to play, in Wittgenstein's expression, a certain "language game," or some relevant part of a language game. Indeed, the problem posed by the ambiguity of ostension might be taken to show that language acquisition cannot be simply a question of each of us, individually and for ourselves, connecting language with the world. As we have already noted, however, this is not Augustine's way out. He supposes that each of us must turn to "the teacher within" for illumination.[4] For him language acquisition is not, then, so much a social skill as it is the ability to make an "inner" connection.

Those who view language acquisition as the development of a social skill can be more relaxed than Augustine is about making sense of even Genesis 1:2: "And the earth was invisible and without form."[5] Here is Augustine puzzling over the expression 'formless matter' in his effort to understand this verse:

> I must confess that when I first heard ['formless matter'] mentioned, I did not understand what it meant, nor did those who told me of it. I used to picture [formless matter] to myself in countless different forms, which means that I did not really picture it at all, because my mind simply conjured up hideous and horrible shapes. They were perversions of the natural order, but shapes nevertheless. I took 'formless' to mean, not something entirely without form, but some shape so monstrous and grotesque that if I were to see it, my senses would recoil

4. It would have been appropriate to call this chapter "Augustine on Illumination." But I want to avoid discussing what is called "the theory of illumination" or "the doctrine of illumination" in Augustine. Augustine uses the light metaphor in a variety of ways. It would take some work to sort these out and distinguish them. As far as I can tell, that project would not clarify the issues I discuss in this book.

5. "Terra erat invisibilis et incomposita" in Augustine's translation; in RSV, "The earth was without form and void."

and my human frailty quail before it. But what I imagined was not truly formless, that is, it was not something bereft of form of any sort. It was formless only by comparison with other more graceful forms. Yet reason told me that if I wished to conceive of something that was formless in the true sense of the word, I should have to picture something deprived of any trace of form whatsoever, and this I was unable to do. (*Confessions*, XII.6)

Augustine decides that the best way out of his problem is to think of radical changes and to conceive something as underlying those changes:

So I gave up trying to find a solution in my imagination, which produced a whole series of pictures of ready-made shapes, shuffling them and rearranging them at will. Instead I turned my attention to material things and looked more closely into the question of their mutability, that is, the means by which they cease to be what they have been and begin to be what they have not been. I suspected that this transition from one form to another might take place by means of an intermediate stage in which they were deprived of all form but were not altogether deprived of existence. (XII.6)

As I said above, the philosopher who supposes language learning to be primarily the acquisition of a social skill can be relaxed even about a case like this. If we learn how to use 'invisible and without form', such a philosopher will say, in ways acceptable to our religious community, we can be satisfied—even though we cannot picture formless void to ourselves or even give ourselves a satisfactory philosophical account of what it might be. For Augustine, though, no such comfort is available. If he is to grasp any truth in this biblical verse he must be able, he supposes, to do it for himself. Since it is of great importance to him to grasp what he supposes is an important truth in this verse, he must slog away to see if he can find its meaning within him. His question is 'Can I find the truth of this verse within me?'—where, often enough, finding the truth within him includes making philosophical sense of the verse.

At the same time, there is in Augustine a remarkable latitudinarianism toward multiple interpretations of the same biblical passage. Without taking back his insistence that "the authority of Scripture should be respected and accepted with the purest faith" (*Confessions* VI.5), he allows that a believer may arrive at strikingly different interpretations of a single verse. Thus Chapter 17 of Book XII of the *Confessions* countenances four alternative interpretations of 'heaven and earth' in Genesis 1:1, in addition to Augustine's own favored interpretation. Chapter 20 offers five possible interpretations of the whole verse, and the next chapter offers five interpretations for "The earth was invisible and without form, and darkness was upon the deep."

Though Augustine always gives reasons for preferring one interpretation to its competitors, he remains surprisingly open to alternatives. His attitude is expressed here:

> All of us who read [the writer's] words do our best to discover and understand what he had in mind, and since we believe that he wrote the truth, we are not so rash as to suppose that he wrote anything which we know or think to be false. Provided, therefore, that each of us tries as best he can to understand in the Holy Scriptures what the writer meant by them, what harm is there if a reader believes what you, the Light of all truthful minds, show him to be the true meaning? It may not even be the meaning which the writer had in mind, and yet he too saw in them a true meaning, different though it may have been from this. (I.18)

෨

What difference does it make whether we take an individualistic approach to meaning, as Augustine does, or a social approach? It might seem that the central issue here concerns our possible beliefs. One might expect a semantic individualist, like Augustine, to say that the truths I can find in Scripture (or in a science textbook) are limited to those whose terms I can interpret satisfactorily for myself. Thus I am not in a position to accept as true the sentence, 'A neutron has mass slightly greater than a proton', or 'The earth was invisible and without form', unless I can interpret satisfactorily the expressions that make up those sentences. And if I cannot do that, then I cannot be led to believe that the earth was without form and void, or that a neutron has mass slightly greater than a proton.

On the social approach, by contrast, my beliefs, under suitable constraints, might include many opinions that I express in terms I cannot satisfactorily interpret for myself. If I am able to defer in appropriate ways to experts on neutrons, or to experts on the formless void, I may be said to hold beliefs whose expressions I cannot interpret satisfactorily for myself.[6]

In fact, Augustine's actual position is rather different from what we might have expected. As we noted in the previous chapter, Augustine insists that belief must precede understanding. "For understanding is the reward of faith. Therefore do not seek to understand in order to believe, but believe that you may understand" (*Homilies on the Gospel of John*, 29.6).

There seems to be a difficulty here. How can I believe, say, that the earth was once invisible and without form, before I understand what that claim means? Augustine's insistence on the temporal priority of faith to understanding applies especially to "higher" or "hidden" truths, as is suggested here:

---

6. As Tyler Burge puts the social thesis, "to a fair degree, mentalistic attribution [including the attribution of beliefs to myself and others] rests not on the subject's having mastered the contents of the attribution, and not on his having behavioral dispositions peculiarly relevant to those contents, but on his having a certain responsibility to communal conventions governing, and conceptions associated with, symbols that he is disposed to use"; see "Individualism and the Mental," *Midwest Studies in Philosophy* 4 (1979), 115.

There are three classes of things to be believed. Some there are which are always believed, and never understood; such is all history, ranging over the temporal doings of man. Others are understood as soon as they are believed; such are all human reasonings, whether on numbers or on any branch of science you please. Thirdly, there are those which are believed and afterwards understood; such are those dealing with divine things. . . . (*Eighty-Three Different Questions*, 48)

Presumably, what Augustine refers to here as history is the mere chronicle of contingent events. We believe that they happen, but we never, he supposes, achieve any real understanding of why.[7]

Concerning the sciences Augustine seems to take the position we should expect of a semantic individualist. On his view, I am not able to believe that the square of the hypotenuse of a right triangle is equal to the sum of the squares of the other two sides, unless I understand what it means to say that. So as soon as I do really believe it, I already, per force, understand it. That leaves the third class of things to be believed—"those which are believed and afterwards understood," presumably such things as formulations of religious doctrine and statements from the Bible. Even with respect to them, Augustine often points out that faith presupposes some minimal understanding of the words that make up the relevant biblical verse or doctrinal statement. In a sermon, Augustine says of his hearers that unless they understand what he is saying, they cannot believe.[8]

When Augustine talks about believing something that one does not understand, he seems to have in mind assenting to some sentence the words of which one understands, even

---

7. Maybe what Augustine means by this remark is illuminated by this comment from a letter: "There are things for which no reason can be given, but that does not mean that there is none, for God made nothing in the universe without a reason" (*Letter* 120).

8. *Sermo* 43.3.4, *Patrologia Latina*, ed. J.-P. Migne, vol. 38 (Paris, 1845).

though one does not understand satisfactorily what the whole sentence means. "For what is believing," he writes, "but consenting to the truth of what is said?" (*On the Spirit and the Letter,* 31.54). But suppose one understands, at least minimally, the words that make up the sentence 'The earth was invisible and without form', and, out of reverence for the Bible, one assents to the assertion. Why not just stop there? Why try to deal with all the philosophical and other puzzles that arise when one tries to give that sentence a satisfactory interpretation? Augustine supposes that, unless I can interpret that sentence satisfactorily for myself, I cannot find "within me" the truth it expresses. And what that means, I take it, is that, although I can believe that the sentence 'The earth was invisible and without form' is true, I cannot grasp its truth. And that is exactly what one would expect a semantic individualist to say.

❧

Augustine's individualistic approach to scriptural exegesis and his preoccupation with what "Truth tells me inwardly in my mind" (*Confessions,* XII.16) balance his confident and substantial appeal to outside authority in seeking lofty and hidden truths. We may need authorities—the Bible, the church—to tell us what is true. But we can, indeed, we must, figure out for ourselves, consulting primarily the teacher within, what a true statement of Scripture or Christian dogma means.

The autobiographical form Augustine's exegesis takes is striking. Instead of disguising his personality or hiding it behind impersonal forms of speech, he presents his searches for adequate interpretations almost as the work of a private detective. These locutions, all from Book XII of the *Confessions,* are typical: "I did not understand what it meant . . ."; "I took 'formless' to mean . . ."; "I was not satisfied with mere theory . . ."; "In my heart, O Lord, I have heard your voice telling me . . ."; "This then, my God, is how I interpret your Scripture . . ."; "I am told by that inner voice . . ."; "I wish to reason a little with those who admit all that your truth tells me inwardly in my mind." Though 'I' questions like these are prominent in Augustine's discussions of meaning and exegesis, 'I*' questions are not. Certainly, as I stated earlier, one might argue that

(5) How can I ever be sure that I* know what 'walking' means?

is an important background question in Augustine's *Concerning the Teacher*. But neither it nor any similar 'I*' question is actually posed in that dialogue by Augustine. And in Augustine's later writings it would be hard to find any 'I*' questions at all that could plausibly be thought to motivate or structure Augustine's discussions of meaning and interpretation.

Descartes's epistemological individualism leads to his rational reconstruction of knowledge and, as I argued in Chapter 11, that reconstruction is both motivated by and structured according to important 'I*' questions. By contrast, Augustine's egocentric approach to language and meaning leads to no similar project. It is, I think, because philosophical individualism in Augustine takes a largely interpretive form, where what is interpreted—Holy Scripture and church doctrine—is taken to be authoritative, that thought's ego fails to play the central role in his thought that it plays in Descartes's. Let me try to clarify this last remark.

To accept the authority of Holy Scripture, let alone the authority of the Catholic church, is to take a stance that is well anchored in what one takes to be an objective, physical world, whose story is thought to extend back well before one was born. Even if one adds, as Augustine certainly does, that each of us individually must interpret that Scripture and those doctrines for ourselves, one is not making any primary place for a point of view from which even the existence of physical objects might be philosophically problematic. As an individual interpreter of Scripture, Augustine does not think of himself as an immaterial mind whose connection to the physical world is philosophically problematic. On the contrary, he thinks of himself as one embodied mind among others—all seeking to interpret sentences written down on quite corporeal scrolls and parchments.

We can appreciate the significance of this point better by taking note of the important differences between the role God plays in Descartes's philosophy and Augustine's. That is the topic of the next chapter.

[13]

God as Guarantor

God plays two especially important roles in Descartes's rational reconstruction of knowledge. First of all, God underwrites for Descartes the rule of clarity and distinctness. "Now, however, I have perceived that God exists, and at the same time I have understood that everything else depends on him, and that he is no deceiver," Descartes writes in Meditation V, "and I have drawn the conclusion that everything which I clearly and distinctly perceive is of necessity true" (AT VII, 70; CSM II, 48). Thus Descartes answers affirmatively the 'I*' question,

(1) Can I conclude that everything I* clearly and distinctly perceive is of necessity true?

And the reasoning he offers to support an affirmative answer to (1) draws on his conclusions about the existence and nature of God, especially his conclusion that God is no deceiver and his idea that God would have to be a deceiver to let him conceive untruths clearly and distinctly.

The second crucial role God plays in Descartes's rational reconstruction of knowledge is as guarantor of the existence of the "external world." "I do not see how God could be understood to be anything but a deceiver," Descartes writes in the middle of Meditation VI, "if the ideas [I have] were transmitted from a source other than corporeal things" (AT VII, 80; CSM II, 55). It is not that Descartes thinks that God's goodness rules out my *ever* being deceived about the source of my ideas. What is ruled out, he thinks, is my having an inclination to believe that they come from corporeal things *and my having no faculty for recognizing otherwise*—which would be my situation if there were in fact no external world, that is, if all life were my dream. By this reasoning Descartes undertakes to answer the question,

(2)   How do I know that not all life is a dream I* am having?

Descartes thinks that he is entitled to rely on God's existence and nature in his rational reconstruction of knowledge—both in backing up the rule of clarity and distinctness and in justifying his belief in the external world—because he has come up with at least two proofs of the existence and nature of God. There is, first of all, the extremely complicated causal argument in Meditation III. And then there is the ontological argument in Meditation V.

Ever since Descartes's own day, commentators have raised questions about whether Descartes is entitled to appeal to the existence and nature of God as a guarantee for his rule of clarity and distinctness. Does Descartes need the rule of clarity and distinctness to prove God's existence and nature, by appeal to which he later seeks to guarantee the rule of clarity and distinctness? If so, it seems, his reasoning is circular. I do not discuss the "Cartesian circle" in this book, nor do I have much more to say about Descartes's proof of the external world. My discussion is limited to pointing out both similarities and differences between the role God plays in Descartes's rational reconstruction of knowledge and the role God plays in the thinking of Augustine. As it turns out, the

differences are intimately bound up with a difference between these two philosophers' respective attitudes toward language, in fact, toward language and skepticism.

Skepticism is clearly important in the thinking of both philosophers. To Augustine it is a threat. But, as we have seen,
what is threatening is global, or universal, skepticism—
skepticism about everything. To put the matter another way,
what is threatening is skepticism as a way of life. If one can
defeat global skepticism, Augustine reasons, then one can
make way for some alternative way of life.

One familiar way to try to defeat universal skepticism is to
turn it on itself. If everything is dubitable, then so is the claim
that everything is dubitable. Augustine's tack is different. He
takes a sample truth, namely, 'I am', and tries to show that
there is something self-defeating in thinking one is deceived
or mistaken about that. In a passage from *On Free Choice of the
Will*, he has Evodius indicate that it is pointless to be afraid
you are deceived in thinking you exist. "If you did not exist,"
he says, "it would be impossible for you to be deceived"
(II.3.7).

In the *City of God*, Augustine begins with the claim to know
that he exists. Against that, he argues, the taunts of the skeptic, "What if you are mistaken?" are futile. Augustine also
claims to know much else besides the fact that he exists. As I
emphasized in Chapters 5 and 7, his concessive response to
the epistemological dream problem consists in pointing out
that there are many things I can know even if I am now
dreaming.

Though the defeat of skepticism as a way of life is important to Augustine, his general position, as we saw in Chapter
11, is that knowledge and understanding need to be coupled
with faith. Thus he has no project of providing a rational
reconstruction of knowledge. He provides a rational defense
of knowledge only in a limited way, by showing that global
skepticism defeats itself when it tries to threaten one's claim to

know that one exists. Recognizing this defeat clears the way for knowledge based on a cooperative relationship between faith and reason.

Descartes's use of skepticism is different. He makes methodological use of skepticism to reconstruct knowledge. Having adopted the method of systematic doubt, I can, according to Descartes, take the failure of the skeptic to call my existence successfully into doubt as a certification of the first principle, 'I am' (or 'I think, therefore I am'). In Descartes, it is not just that skepticism undermines itself and so discredits itself; nor is it that skepticism must break down somewhere. It is rather that skepticism can be used to certify the foundation stone for a rational reconstruction of knowledge. Skepticism can thus be turned into an engine that generates a basis for reconstructed knowledge.

Since Augustine has no such project as the rational reconstruction of knowledge, God cannot play for him a role entirely parallel to the role He plays for Descartes. But is there in Augustine even a partial parallel? There is an argument for the existence of God in Augustine's *On Free Choice of the Will* II.15.39. Although it is not an impressive argument, it has some interest in the present context. Augustine gets his interlocutor, Evodius, to admit:

(3)　x is God if and only if x is more excellent than our minds and nothing is more excellent than x.

He then tries to establish:

(4)　Truth exists and it is more excellent than our minds.

From these two premises he concludes:

(5)　Something is God (i.e., God exists).

His idea is that either nothing is more excellent than truth, so that, since truth is more excellent than our minds, truth itself is God; or else something is more excellent even than truth, in which case it (or, we could add, something even more excellent than it) is God.

The relevance of this argument to our present concerns is that it uses the claim that truth is something more excellent than our minds and is at least a candidate for being God. If there could be no knowledge without truth (perhaps because '*x* knows that *p*' entails 'it is true that *p*') then, according to (3) and (4), there can be no knowledge without God.

Is this at all close to Descartes? Not really. We do not have here anything like Descartes's appeal to God's faithfulness to underwrite our reliance on clear and distinct ideas. At most we have an argument for proving the existence of God from the fact of knowledge, not one for proving the fact of knowledge from the existence and nature of God.

Is there anywhere in Augustine anything like Descartes's appeal to God's faithfulness to underwrite our reliance on clear and distinct ideas? One might suppose that what in the Augustinian tradition has come to be called the "doctrine of divine illumination" is such an appeal. The divine light, Augustine says, makes possible our apprehension of the truths of reason. This talk of the light of reason as being a divine light, one might suppose, is like Descartes's claim that God backs up our applications of the criterion of clarity and distinctness.

I am myself skeptical about whether we can find anything behind Augustine's metaphors of divine illumination that deserves to be called a philosophical doctrine.[1] But it is certainly true that Augustine sometimes describes God as the light by

---

1. I agree with Etienne Gilson's rather negative assessment of the attempts in the Augustinian tradition to find a philosophical doctrine of illumination in Augustine; see his patient discussion in *The Christian Philosophy of Saint Augustine* (New York: Random House, 1960), 77–96.

which we make true judgments of reason, as in this passage from his commentary on Genesis: "For the Light is God Himself, whereas the soul is a creature. . . . And when [the soul] tries to behold the Light, it trembles in its weakness and finds itself unable to do so. Yet from this source comes all the understanding it is able to entertain" (*The Literal Meaning of Genesis*, XII.31.59).

The suggested parallel with Descartes, is not, however, as close as one might have thought. In describing God as the divine light, Augustine here and elsewhere certainly credits God with making it possible for us to know or understand whatever it is we know or understand. But Augustine never asks anything that resembles at all closely Descartes's 'I*' question from Meditation III, "Do I now therefore also know what is required for my being certain about anything?" (AT VII, 34; CSM II, 24). He does not try to specify a condition c such that one can know that whenever c is satisfied one is justified in taking oneself to be seeing a truth in the divine light. To do that would be, as we said in Chapter 11, to commit oneself to what is these days called "internalism" in epistemology, and Augustine is not in this sense an internalist.

The larger point is that Augustine never makes the Cartesian resolution, 'I shall guide myself in the search for all that I* can know'. And so he never takes on the project of trying to say, from the point of view of his thought's ego, how he can be sure of knowing whatever it is he thinks he knows. Augustine certainly does acknowledge God's role in his being able to know what he knows. But he does not require that God back up any rule or criterion he appeals to in justifying his claim to know what he claims to know.

ě❧

There is a way in which God's trustworthiness does, for Augustine, underwrite philosophical inquiry; but it is totally different from the way in which Descartes relies on God. A familiar kind of philosophical question has the form, 'How is it possible that p?' The cadence may strike us as Kantian. Kant asked, "How is synthetic a priori knowledge possible?" (i.e., how is it possible that there is synthetic a priori knowledge?). But raising a question that can be put easily and naturally in this form is as old as philosophy. Plato's Socrates asks, in effect, "How is it possible that one desires bad things?" (*Meno*) and "How is it possible that one does what one knows one ought not to be doing?" (*Gorgias*). In both cases, Plato's answer is that it is not possible, although he explains that we can seem to desire bad things and do what we seem to know we ought not to be doing. Aristotle, on the other hand, tries to explain (in ways that are still subject to interpretation and debate) how it *is* possible to be doing what one knows one ought not to be doing.

Questions of the form, 'How is it possible that p?' may be asked either safely or with risk. If they are asked safely, the presumption that p is not put in jeopardy to one's ability to give a satisfactory account of how it is possible that p. If they are asked with risk, however, then one's inability to explain how it is possible that p must be taken as a reason to doubt that p; moreover, an account of how it is *not* possible that p must be taken as a reason to deny that p.

In a stimulating and provocative article, M. F. Burnyeat argues that the practice of asking philosophical questions safely is a modern innovation. In particular, it is his contention that "insulation," as he calls it, is Kant's invention. This is the way Burnyeat introduces the idea of insulation:

Nowadays, if a philosopher finds he cannot answer the philosophical question 'What is time?' or 'Is time real?', he applies for a research grant to work on the problem during the next year's sabbatical. He does not suppose that the arrival of next year is actually in doubt. Alternatively, he may agree that any puzzlement about the nature of time, or any argument for doubting the reality of time, is in fact a puzzlement about, or an argument for doubting, the truth of the proposition that next year's sabbatical will come, but contend that this is of course a strictly theoretical or philosophical worry, not a worry that needs to be reckoned with in the ordinary business of life. Either way he *insulates* his ordinary first order judgements from the effects of his philosophizing.[2]

Burnyeat argues in some detail, and this is the primary focus of his discussion, that neither Sextus Empiricus nor any other ancient skeptics insulated their ordinary beliefs from the conclusions of philosophical argumentation. After a much briefer discussion, he maintains that not Socrates, or Plato, or Aristotle, or Descartes, or Berkeley, or even Hume practiced insulation either. Thus a familiar modern attitude toward philosophy, and toward philosophical skepticism, is, according to Burnyeat, no older than Kant, "who persuaded philosophy that one can be, simultaneously and without contradiction, an empirical realist and a transcendental idealist."[3]

I suggest, on the contrary, that insulation is characteristic of Augustine. Early in his life, perhaps at the time of *Against the Academics,* philosophical skepticism is for him an urgent threat, something to be refuted before one is in position to take up another alternative. Perhaps there is no insulation there. In his other early writings, for example *On Free Choice of the Will,* which I referred to earlier in this chapter, there seems to be interest in philosophical argumentation as a sort of scaffolding for theology. It is hard to be clear about what is philosophically at risk in these works. In any case, interest in that sort of project soon dies out. At the same time, Augustine's arguments against Academic skepticism become more professional and less existential. And belief in the divine inspiration of Holy Scripture turns rock solid. Au-

---

2. "The Sceptic in His Place and Time," in *Philosophy in History,* ed. R. Rorty, J. B. Schneewind, and Q. Skinner (Cambridge: Cambridge University Press, 1984), 225–254, quotation from 225.
3. Ibid., 250.

gustine's ruminatively philosophical temperament survives alongside a total confidence in divine revelation. In the *City of God*, Augustine's last large-scale work, there is still a place, admittedly, for speculative theology. "It is a great achievement," he writes, "and no everyday matter, that man in his speculation should go beyond the created universe, having examined it, both in its material and immaterial aspects, and found it mutable, and arrive at the immutable being of God" (XI.2). But the importance of such "speculation" is now taken to be very small. For, as Augustine says later in the same chapter,

> the mind of man, the natural seat of his reason and understanding, is itself weakened by long-standing faults which darken it. It is too weak to cleave to that changeless light and to enjoy it; it is too weak even to endure that light. It must be renewed and healed day after day so as to become capable of such felicity. And so the mind had to be trained and purified by faith; and in order to give man's mind greater confidence in its journey towards the truth along the way of faith, God the Son of God, who is himself the Truth, took manhood without abandoning his godhead, and thus established and founded this faith, so that man might have a path to man's god through the man who was God. (XI.2)

Such devaluation of the worth of unaided reason and such depreciation of the promises of systematic philosophy are hardly unusual in Augustine's mature writing. Already in the *Confessions* we find him admitting that "we are too weak to discover the truth by reason alone and for this reason need the authority of [the] sacred books" (VI.5). And about his own book, *Of True Religion*, written a year or so before the *Confessions*, he writes almost two decades later to his good friend, Evodius, as follows: "If you would review [that work] and look into it, you would never think that reason can prove the necessity of God's existence, or that by reasoning it can ever be established that God must necessarily exist" (*Letters*, 162).

Right after the lamentation on the frailty of unaided reason from the *City of God* (XI.2), Augustine stakes out his claim for the authority of Scripture. Christ, the Mediator, he writes, "also inspired the Scripture, which is regarded as canonical and of *supreme authority* and to which we give credence concerning all those truths we ought to know and yet, of ourselves, are unable to learn" (XI.3, emphasis added). What scope is there then for philosophy, when the fruits of philosophical speculation are thought to be so meager and unreliable, and when the Bible as the divinely inspired word of God is taken to be supremely authoritative and so nearly self-sufficient? The answer is that there is plenty of room for philosophy, considered now as the reflection on, and analysis of, the *meaning* of all sorts of statements whose *truth* is thought to be beyond doubt. Those statements include claims actually stated in the Bible; theological doctrines based in some way on the Bible; and expressions of ordinary, everyday beliefs, most of which could be conceived as background beliefs for scriptural statements and theological doctrines.

For biblical statements, Augustine early on formulates the distinction between questions about their truth and questions about their meaning, as in this passage from the *Confessions:*

> I realize that when a message is delivered to us in words, truthful though the messenger be, two sorts of disagreement may arise. We may disagree either as to the truth of the message itself or as to the messenger's meaning. It is one thing to ask what is true about the manner of creation, and another to ask what Moses, who was so good a servant to the family of your faithful, meant those who read or heard his words to understand by them. (XII.23)

The biblical sentence Augustine has under discussion is Genesis 1:1: "In the beginning God made heaven and earth." As we have noted in earlier chapters, Augustine comments on this sentence in many of his most important works. It leads him to wonderful reflections, many of them philosophical, on time and creation. It inspires him to formulate at least three different theories of time. Even in a single discussion he may allow several different ways of understanding this verse. What he never doubts, apparently, is that the statement is true. Right after the passage above he entertains two interpretations and concludes, "Nevertheless, whether this great man [Moses] had one of these two meanings in mind when he wrote those words, or was thinking of some other meaning which I have not set down here, I am quite sure that he saw the truth and expressed it accordingly" (XII.24).

We have seen that Augustine assigns "supreme authority" to Scripture. Certainly he also says, for example, in his *Christian Instruction*, that "it is necessary that we become meek through piety so that we do not contradict Divine Scripture" (I.7.9). But it would be wrong to think of Augustine as a literalistic exegete; quite the opposite is true. Here are two passages—both of them from Augustine's *The Literal Meaning of Genesis* and one of them cited by Galileo more than a millennium later[4]—that show something of the hermeneutic and philosophical sophistication with which Augustine approaches the task of biblical exegesis:

> When they are able, from reliable evidence, to prove some fact of physical science, we shall show that it is not contrary to our Scripture. But when they produce from any of their books a theory contrary to Scripture, and therefore contrary to the Catholic faith, either we shall have some ability to demonstrate that it is absolutely false, or at least we ourselves will hold it so without any shadow of doubt. (I.21.41)

4. See "Galileo's Letter to the Grand Duchess Christina (1615)," in *The Galileo Affair: A Documentary History*, ed. Maurice A. Finocchiaro (Berkeley: University of California Press, 1989), 87–118. I owe this reference to Edwin McCann.

But someone may ask: "Is not Scripture opposed to those who hold that heaven is spherical, when it says, *who stretches out heaven like a skin?*" [*Psalm* 103.2.] Let it be opposed indeed if their statement is false. The truth is rather in what God reveals than in what groping men surmise. But if they are able to establish their doctrine with proofs that cannot be denied, we must show that this statement of Scripture about the skin is not opposed to the truth of their conclusions. If it were, it would be opposed also to Sacred Scripture itself in another passage where it says that heaven is suspended like a vault. . . . But if it is necessary, as it surely is, to interpret these two passages so that they are shown not to be contradictory but to be reconcilable, it is also necessary that both of these passages should not contradict the theories that may be supported by true evidence. . . . (II.9.21)

Not only do specific scriptural verses require interpretation, so do doctrines culled from scriptural verses, such as the doctrine that God is Father, Son, and Holy Spirit. In the *Christian Instruction* Augustine gives this statement of the doctrine of the divine Trinity:

Thus, there are Father, Son, and Holy Ghost. Each of these individually is God. At the same time They are all one God. Each of Them individually comprises the fullness of the divine substance. At the same time They are all only one substance. The Father is neither the Son nor the Holy Ghost; the Son is neither the Father nor the Holy Ghost; the Holy Ghost is neither the Father nor the Son. The Father is only the Father; the Son, only the Son; the Holy Ghost, only the Holy Ghost. All Three have the same eternity, the same immutability, the same majesty, the same power. In the Father resides unity, in the Son equality, and in the Holy Ghost the perfect union of unity and equality. These three qualities are all one because of the Father, all equal because of the Son, and all united because of the Holy Ghost. (I.5.5)

In the next chapter Augustine asks whether he has said anything "worthy of God" and replies negatively. He says that he has done "nothing but wish to speak." He considers calling God ineffable, but demurs: "God should not be spoken of even as ineffable, because, when we say this word, we are saying something about Him. There is some contradiction of terms, since, if that is ineffable which cannot be spoken of, a thing is not ineffable which can be called ineffable" (I.6.6) The passage is striking. It may remind a twentieth-century philosopher of such recent objects of attention as the liar paradox and Russell's paradox. In fact there is an easy proof, almost but not quite given in the above passage, that nothing is ineffable. Suppose something were. Then it could be described as ineffable. So it could be described. So it would not be ineffable. Therefore nothing is ineffable. Of course, one could try inventing a new term, 'noneffable', for "something indescribable in every way except by saying it is noneffable." A mystic might be content to call God noneffable, but a philosophically astute mystic might balk. After all, the term to be defined appears in the definiens.

In any case, Augustine goes another route. He first suggests silence. Then he falls back on saying, in the *Christian Instruction* anyway, that even the elaborate trinitarian formula quoted above is not *worthy* of God.

Years later, in *The Trinity*, Augustine first grounds in Scripture a somewhat sanitized version of the doctrine of the divine Trinity (he deletes, for example, the claim that God is a substance; VII.5.10). Then he spends the last eight books of that work providing analogies for the divine Trinity from the human mind (in, for example, the trinity of memory, understanding, and will). *The Trinity*, especially, could be said to concern the question, 'How is it possible that God is three in one?' The question is asked safely rather than with risk; the truth of the claim that God is indeed three in one, as founded in Scripture, is never put in jeopardy to Augustine's ability to provide a satisfactory analysis of it. Though he pursues the analogies so thoroughly that the result is an interesting treatise in the philosophy of mind, he remains diffident about the capacity of these psychological analogies to illuminate the doctrine of the divine Trinity.

Here is another example. Among Augustine's contemporaries the question of whether telling a lie might ever be morally or religiously permissible, perhaps even obligatory, was hotly debated. Augustine addresses this issue in many of his works, but he devotes two treatises wholly to the topic of lying. In both of them he condemns lying, even when the lie might thought to bring about some greater good. He bases his condemnation on the biblical commandment, "You shall not bear false witness!" And in both treatises he views lying as a kind of self-defilement.

The first of the two treatises devoted solely to this topic, *Lying*, begins with a philosophically provocative discussion of the nature of lying. Augustine is inclined to suppose that

(6)   A person A lies in saying that p if and only if (i) it is in fact false that p, (ii) A believes it is false that p, and (iii) A says that p with the intention of deceiving someone.

But against the necessity of these conditions he considers (a) the case of someone who believes false what is in fact true, so that the first condition is not fulfilled, though there is still an intention to deceive; (b) the case of someone who, hoping and expecting to be disbelieved, says what is false to get someone to believe the truth; and (c) the case of someone who, expecting to be disbelieved, tells the truth in order to deceive another (like the fabled traveling salesman in old Russia, whose competitor charges, "You're just telling me you're going to Minsk so that I'll think you're going to Pinsk, when you really *are* going to Minsk, you dirty liar!"). Augustine seems uncertain as to what to do with these putative counterexamples. He contents himself with insisting that the three conditions are jointly sufficient and leaves undecided whether they are severally necessary (*Lying*, 4.5).

How is it possible to know that it is always wrong to lie, one might protest, when we are not clear about what conditions are necessary for something to count as a lie? Augustine's reply is that we do not know that lying is wrong by appeal to some other general idea or principle, from which we have deduced the prohibition against lying. We have simply read in the Bible, "You shall not bear false witness," and we know that what is claimed in the Bible is true, whatever exactly it may turn out to mean.[5] The framework of a scripturally based belief system, held constant in faith, seems to free Augustine to pursue other philosophical questions safely as well. He seems willing and able to ask, "How is it possible that *p*?" safely, even when the belief that *p* is a commonsense belief that one would not naturally appeal to Scripture to justify. For example, in Book X of the *Confessions,* in the long and fascinating discussion of *memoria,* Augustine stumbles onto this problem: "My memory also contains my feelings [*affectiones animi*], not in the same way as they are present to the mind when it experiences them, but in a quite different way that is in keeping with the special powers of the memory. For even when I am unhappy I can remember times when I was cheerful, and when I am cheerful I can remember past unhappiness" (X.14).

The question is 'How is it possible that even when I am unhappy I can remember times when I was cheerful?' This is a difficult question for Augustine, since he understands remembering, in cases like this, as perceiving a mental representation. The representation is a likeness, he thinks, of what it represents. But how could a representation of cheerfulness

---

5. There is much more to be said about Augustine's various discussions of lying. Christopher Kirwan's treatment of these matters in *Augustine,* 196–204, is especially helpful. As Kirwan makes clear, Augustine needs to explain away the biblical passages in which lying is apparently condoned. Furthermore, Augustine does try in various ways to render the biblical prohibition against lying acceptable.

resemble cheerfulness without being itself a bit of cheerfulness? If it were a bit of cheerfulness, though, one could not
remember being cheerful, it seems, without being cheerful.

Sometimes, of course, remembering better days does cheer
one up. But sometimes it makes one only more resentful and
morose. So remembering cheerful times is not in and of itself
a way of being cheerful. But how can it not be? "We might
say," Augustine suggests, "that the memory is a sort of stomach for the mind, and that joy or sadness are like sweet or
bitter food. When this food is committed to the memory, it is
as though it had passed into the stomach where it can remain
but also loses its taste" (X.14).

Alas! The analogy fails to help. On this analogy, remembering would be regurgitating one's food. But regurgitation
would not be memory without recognition of what was re-
gurgitated. And then the problem recurs. Surely in tasting
the joy of one's past experience one would be joyful. But, as
we have admitted, this need not be so.

Since, as Augustine supposes, memory yields representations that give us the very meaning of emotion words like
'cheer', 'sorrow', and 'fear', Augustine's account of meaning is
in trouble over this problem. "For if we had to experience
sorrow or fear every time we mentioned these emotions," he
admits, "no one would be willing to speak of them. Yet we
could not speak of them at all unless we could find in our
memory not only the sounds of their names, which we retain
as images imprinted on the memory by the senses of the body,
but also the ideas of the emotions themselves"(X.14).

As far as I can see, Augustine never solves this problem. Yet
he does not conclude that, when we are unhappy, we cannot
remember times when we were cheerful without becoming
cheerful. Nor does he conclude that one cannot use the words
'sorrow' or 'fear' without becoming sorrowful or afraid. He
does his philosophy with insulation. His attitude toward this
problem seems entirely in keeping with that of a modern
professional philosopher who applies for a grant to work on

the question, without in any way supposing that the amount of fear or joy there is in the world may be better estimated after the problem has been solved.

❧

God is, we have seen, a guarantor for Augustine fully as much as for Descartes, but in a very different way. God does not, for Augustine, guarantee the rule of clarity and distinctness; Augustine uses no such rule. Nor does God's faithfulness underwrite Augustine's solution to the problem of the external world; Augustine recognizes no such problem. But God, through what Augustine unwaveringly (at least unwaveringly after his conversion) takes to be his Holy Word, does provide Augustine with an indefinitely large stock of things to be believed. More particularly, God supplies him with an indefinitely large number of statements to be accepted, plus a large supply of what we might call "background beliefs." The truth of those statements is not, for him, in doubt; their meaning is. And the background beliefs, though not hallowed, are at least protected.

Augustine's characteristically philosophical aim is something more modest than the rational reconstruction of knowledge. It is the reflective appreciation of how it can be the case that p, for philosophically interesting and problematic claims that p. That aim strikes many of us modern philosophers as more up-to-date, more like what drives discussions in our own philosophy journals and in hotel rooms during annual meetings of the American Philosophical Association, than does the aim of the "father of modern philosophy."

Lying behind Augustine's search for understanding is the idea that only through a reflective appreciation of how it can be the case that p can I find the truth that p "within me." Where the claim that p is of great religious or moral significance—as with the claim that God made heaven and earth or that we should never tell lies—finding that truth within me will certainly be of central importance to me, even when, without that understanding, I have no doubt that somehow or other it is true.

Burnyeat is right to say that insulating skepticism is a characteristically post-Kantian phenomenon in philosophy. One thinks, for example, of G. E. Moore's admission: "I am not at all sceptical as to the *truth* of such propositions as 'The earth has existed for many years past.' . . . on the contrary, I hold that we all know, with certainty, many such propositions to be true. But I am very sceptical as to what, in certain respects, the *analysis* of such propositions is."[6] Moore's restriction of skepticism to the *analysis* of accepted truths is in many ways like Augustine's freedom to be skeptical about the *meaning* of Biblical dogmas and what I have called "background beliefs" associated with them—all the while holding firmly and unquestioningly to their truth. Similar also is the view of many of our contemporaries that natural science is our best guide to what is true, though philosophy needs to try to say what the truths of science mean. To modern insulators, whether they be devotees of common sense, of ordinary language, or of natural science, it may be ironic that Augustine's basis for insulation should be something so thoroughly old-fashioned as his faith in the trustworthiness of God and the inerrancy of Scripture. But then, irony is no barrier to truth.

By standing behind the rational reconstruction of knowledge, God helps liberate Descartes from epistemological ego isolation. God is, in an important way, Descartes's surety. What Augustine thinks of himself as owing to God, epistemologically, is rather different. Augustine supposes that God, by assuring us of the truth of Scripture, helps us get beyond the meager stock of truths we can use unaided philosophy to prove. The remaining job Augustine uses philosophy for, after he has established 'I am', 'I know that I am', and the like, is to

6. "A Defence of Common Sense," in *Philosophical Papers* (London: Allen and Unwin, 1959), 52.

help him see how the truths of Scripture can in fact be true—
that is, to help him understand those truths. Augustine describes the process of coming to understand God's truths as
finding those truths "within," where, he says, Christ is his
inner teacher. When we see what is involved, for Augustine,
in finding those truths within him, we can only conclude that
Christ, the inner teacher, must be a good philosopher.

[14]

Thought's Ego

Descartes's most famous work, the *Meditations on First Philosophy*, is a soliloquy of the purest sort. It presents the reflections of a solitary thinker who, before those reflections come to an end, has taken seriously the possibility that he might be alone in existing, that is, that solipsism might be true. We readers overhear his soliloquy in such a way that we can make his thoughts our own. In thinking our own version of his thoughts, we are, each of us, to ask ourselves, among other ego-isolating questions, the most ego-isolating question of all: 'How do I know that not all my experience is just a dream I* am having?'

Descartes's second most famous work, the *Discourse on the Method*, is an autobiography. It too is written in a style that invites each of us readers to think our own individual version of Descartes's thoughts after him. Each of us is thus to have, individually, for ourselves, the thought, "All the things that [have] ever entered my mind [are] no more true than the illusions of my dreams" (AT VI, 32; CSM I, 127).

Although Descartes's other main philosophical work, the *Principles of Philosophy*, was not written in the style of a soliloquy or an autobiography, it begins with this prescriptive paragraph:

Since we began life as infants, and made various judgements
concerning the things that can be perceived by the senses before we had the full use of our reason, there are many precon-
ceived opinions that keep us from knowledge of the truth. It
seems that the only way of freeing ourselves from these opinions is to make the effort, once in the course of our life, to
doubt everything which we find to contain even the smallest
suspicion of uncertainty. (AT VIIIA, 5; CSM I, 193)

By admonition, then, rather than by example, the *Principles*
too invites each of us, individually, to conduct a philosophical
inquiry from the perspective of thought's ego. In the course
of doing that, we are each to have the isolation-threatening
thought that "there seem to be no marks by means of which
we can with certainty distinguish being asleep from being
awake" (AT VIIIA, 6; CSM I, 194).

The central place of thought's ego in Descartes's philosophy
is thus clinched by the metaphysical dream problem. But it is
also confirmed by other aspects of Descartes's thought, most
strikingly, perhaps, by his epistemological internalism. Readers of each of these treatises are to ask themselves individually, "Do I know what is required for me* to be justifiably
certain about something?" And they are to answer with the
rule of clarity and distinctness. In this way they are each to
discover, within themselves, the basis for what they can legitimately claim to know.

Like Descartes, Augustine wrote philosophy in the form of
a soliloquy. In fact, he wrote a work entitled *The Soliloquies.*
"For long I had been turning over in my mind many various
thoughts," this work begins. It continues, "Suddenly someone
spoke to me, whether it was myself or someone else from
without or from within I know not. Indeed, to know that, is
my main endeavour. At any rate someone, Let us call him
Reason, said to me . . . " (I.1.1). From this beginning we might
expect an inquiry conducted by thought's ego, that is, organized and directed by 'I*' questions. But that never happens.

From Augustine's statement of the topic to be discussed one might also be encouraged to expect that thought's ego would soon take over the inquiry. "For many days," Augustine writes, "I had been earnestly seeking to know myself and my chief good and what evil was to be shunned" (I.1.1). Although Augustine does not put it this way, one could perhaps say that, by implication, Augustine is here making the Cartesian-type resolution, "I will let reason guide me* in the search to know myself* and my* chief good and what evil I* should shun."

Reason tells Augustine to write down his thoughts. "These thoughts must not be dictated," he warns; "for they require complete solitude" (I.1.1). Epistemological privacy, it seems, is to be respected. But the privacy of that reflective solitude is almost immediately shattered by two thoughts. First, Reason admonishes Augustine to pray to God for health and help in his inquiry. Then Reason adds this thought: "[W]rite this down that you may become more spirited in your quest. Then briefly summarize your conclusions in a few short theses. Do not look to attract a multitude of readers. This will be sufficient for the few who share your fellowship" (I.1.1). The mention of 'readers' here, whether they be "a multitude" or just "the few," certainly destroys the vicarious sense of metaphysical isolation. No doubt Descartes too thought about his readership when he wrote down his meditations. But any thoughts he may have had about his readers remain outside the "story line" of the treatise itself. In fact, how the thinker of the *Meditations* knows there even exists an external world of, as it may be, readers of books is a question to be raised *within* the inquiry.

The lengthy prayer to God that comes next in Augustine's *Soliloquies* contains, among its many metaphysical commitments, these noteworthy items: (i) God exists; (ii) it is through God that all things that would not exist by themselves come into existence; (iii) God created the world out of nothing; (iv) it is through God that the world, even with "its sinister aspects," is perfect; and (v) God is the Truth by whom all true things are true. The list could easily be extended. Each of these commitments belongs to the "view from nowhere" rather than to the view from the "here" of thought's ego.

The rest of Book I of the *Soliloquies* could be said to be an effort to develop a better understanding of these commitments and others like them. Yet this effort at reflective understanding does not amount to an attempt to prove such statements or to show how they fit into a reconstruction of what one can know. Moreover—and this is the point I want to emphasize—'I*' questions play no significant role in the discussion.

Book II might seem to be different. Although it too begins with a prayer, this time the prayer is mercifully short. "O God," prays Augustine, "who art ever the same, let me know myself and thee" (II.1.1). There then follows this exchange with Reason:

> REASON: You who wish to know yourself, do you know that you exist?
> AUGUSTINE: I do.
> REASON: How do you know?
> AUGUSTINE: That I do not know.
>
> .
> .
> .
>
> REASON: You know that you think?
> AUGUSTINE: I do.
> REASON: Then it is true that you think?
> AUGUSTINE: It is true.
>
> (II.1.1)

Here, at last, we encounter two real 'I*' questions: 'Do I know that I* exist?' and 'Do I know that I* think?' But they are passed over remarkably quickly. In fact, they get no further discussion at all. They could hardly be said to structure the inquiry. One can only conclude that, despite its literary form, and despite the encouragement it gives to solitary reflection,

Augustine's *Soliloquies* is not directed by or structured according to thought's ego.

Is the situation different in the *Confessions?* In literary form, the *Confessions* is an address, or an allocution, directed to God. It is, of course, meant to be read by others. And it is, no doubt, meant to encourage self-examination in its readers analogous to the examination Augustine conducts of himself throughout its pages. Yet thought's ego plays no major role in any of this. Of the six 'I*' questions I have given special emphasis to in my discussion, only the moral dream problem ('Am I responsible for what I* do in my dreams?') turns up in the *Confessions.* It takes up exactly one of the forty-three chapters of one of its thirteen books. Thought's ego could hardly be said to be prominent in the work as a whole.

Among Augustine's many writings, it is no doubt his *The Trinity* that is most taken up with the topics we have been discussing in this study. In Book VIII Augustine presents his version of the problem of other minds. In Book X he asks what the mind can be certain that it* is. And in Book XV he asks whether I can be mistaken in thinking that I* live. Still, the *The Trinity* is not a soliloquy, an autobiography, a confession, or a set of meditations. It is a theological treatise aimed at clarifying the Christian doctrine of the Trinity. The last half of it seeks to find in the human mind various analogies to the threefold nature of God. As I try to bring out shortly, thought's ego does play an important role in the last half of *The Trinity,* especially in Book X. But it is not true that the discussion, even in Book X, is organized or directed from that point of view.

୬

The two 'I*' questions Augustine most often considers are, 'Can I be certain that I* exist?' and 'How do I know whether I* am now dreaming?' With each one, the point up for discussion is skepticism. One's specimen knowledge that one* exists is offered as a refutation of Academic skepticism. And the epistemological dream problem is taken to be a threat that must be answered with the immunity response (see Chapter 5) so that we can proceed with our claims to knowledge without the danger that the dream threat will undermine everything. True, the treatises in which these two 'I*' questions make their appearance—for example, the *Soliloquies*, the *City of God*, and *The Trinity* for the first, *Against the Academics* and *The Immortality of the Soul* for the second—are not otherwise organized or directed by thought's ego. Augustine's use of 'I*' questions is thus less extensive than Descartes's. Nevertheless, it is important in Augustine's rejection of skepticism.

The other central role 'I*' questions play in Augustine's philosophy is to adumbrate a concept of mind. It is that role to which I devote most of the rest of this final chapter. In developing this discussion, I return to the ideas from Chapter 4, now to be viewed in the light of later discussion, especially that of the metaphysical dream problem in Chapter 6.

Augustine talks about his inquiry into the nature of mind this way: "But since we are investigating the nature of the mind, let us not take into consideration any knowledge that is obtained from without, through the senses of the body, and consider more attentively the principle which we have laid down: that every mind knows and is certain concerning itself" (*Trinity*, X.10.14). One may well wonder what is to be included in the claim that "every mind knows and is certain concerning itself." The surrounding discussion makes clear that knowing itself and being certain concerning itself include knowing that it exists or, as Augustine prefers to say in *The Trinity*, that it "lives."[1]

1. As I remarked in Chapter 4, 'lives' and 'life' in Augustine are not in general to be given a specifically biological sense; rather, they are to be

Two sections later Augustine makes clear that he includes in his claim that "every mind knows and is certain concerning itself" the idea that every mind knows its substance. He tries to get at the nature of the mind's substance by both negative and positive means. Positively, he assigns to the mind those features of himself that satisfy both these conditions: (i) he cannot doubt that they belong to him, and (ii) concerning them he need not "take into consideration any knowledge that is obtained from without through the senses of the body." Negatively, he excludes from the substance of the mind anything that the mind itself is uncertain belongs to it*. This negative requirement is especially interesting and important.

On the positive side,

> who would doubt that he lives, remembers, understands, wills, thinks, knows, and judges? For even if he doubts, he lives; if he doubts, he remembers why he doubts; if he doubts, he understands that he doubts; if he doubts, he wishes to be certain; if he doubts, he thinks; if he doubts, he knows that he does not know; if he doubts, he judges that he ought not to consent rashly. Whoever then doubts about anything else ought never to doubt about all of these; for if they were not, he would be unable to doubt about anything at all. (*Trinity*, X.10.14)

Since we cannot reasonably doubt that we live, remember, understand, will, think, know, and judge, condition (i) is satisfied. Since to determine all this we need "not take into consideration any knowledge that is obtained from without through the senses of the body," condition (ii) is also satisfied. Therefore, these functions and activities can be said to belong to the mind's own substance.

Could the mind be something material? As Augustine

---

understood in the sense of the question, 'Is there life after death?' Presumably that question does not mean, 'Is there biological, or organic, life after death?' but rather, 'Will we survive our deaths?' 'Will we continue to exist after our deaths?'

points out, some philosophers have supposed this. "Those," he says, "who regard the mind either as a body or as the combination or harmony of the body" take living, remembering, understanding, willing, thinking, and so on to be activities of this body. Their idea, he says, is that air or fire or some other body "would be the substance which they call the mind, while the understanding [thinking, and so on] would be in this body as its quality . . ." (X.10.15) As I tried to bring out in Chapter 4, Augustine seeks to refute the idea that the mind is something corporeal by appeal to this principle:

(1)   If x knows the substance of y, then, for any stuff z, if y is z, then x is certain whether y is z.

Thus,

(2)   If the mind knows its own substance, then, for any stuff z, if the mind is z, then the mind is certain whether it is z.

The mind, he reasons, is *not* certain whether it is air or fire or any other body; therefore, it is none of these. It is therefore an immaterial being.

Augustine's reasoning about the mind incorporates many implicit 'I*' questions—for example, 'Can I doubt that I* live (exist)?' and 'Can I doubt that I* think?' But it also makes use of various 'it*' questions, such as, 'Is the mind certain about itself*?' and 'Is the mind certain whether it* is air?' I want now to link the importance of these 'it*' questions to the *absence* in Augustine of the metaphysical dream problem. To do that, I need to return briefly to Descartes for an important comparison.

As I reconstructed his reasoning in Chapter 4, Descartes makes use of the following premises in arguing for the real distinction between mind and body:

(3)   I can clearly and distinctly understand myself apart
       from my body.
(4)   If I can clearly and distinctly understand x apart from
       y, then x and y are capable of being separated by God.
(5)   If x and y are capable of being separated by God, x
       and y are really distinct.

From them, he concludes,

(6)   My body and I are really distinct.

Part of what Descartes counts on to support (3) is his description of himself in Meditation II as something that doubts,
understands, affirms, denies, is willing, is unwilling, imagines,
and has sensory perceptions. But a crucial part of what is
meant to give (3) plausibility is the fact that he can describe
himself so clearly *while taking seriously the possibility that all life is
his dream* and *before he has established that there even exist bodies*. In
other words, the metaphysical dream problem plays a crucial
role in rendering (3) plausible for Descartes.

What about Augustine? He does not pose the metaphysical
dream problem. So how does he move from saying, not just
that living, remembering, understanding, willing, thinking,
and so on belong to me, and, more particularly, to my mind,
but that my mind is an immaterial entity distinct from my
body? The answer is that Augustine does it by considering,
not only what I can be certain about concerning myself*, but
what the mind can be certain of concerning itself*. Augustine
does not have to say, "I am not certain whether I* am a body,
and therefore I am not one." In fact, he seems to take it for
granted that, in this life anyway, he is a soul in a body. Following St. Paul, he even supposes that in the resurrection he will
be a soul in a transformed body, a spiritual body, which he
thinks of as an ideally efficient body that will come to replace
the old sluggish and arthritic body we are used to: "[W]hen
the soul is made equal to the angels and receives again this

body, no longer a natural body but a spiritual one because of the transformation that is to be, it will have the perfect measure of its being, obeying and commanding, vivified and vivifying with such a wonderful ease that what was once its burden will be its glory" (*The Literal Meaning of Genesis*, XII.35.68)

Augustine does not, then, even think to ask, "Am *I* certain whether I* am a body?" Instead his question becomes, 'What is *the mind* certain and uncertain that *it** is?' Since the mind is certain of itself* and knows its* own substance and yet is uncertain whether it* is fire or water or anything bodily, we may conclude, Augustine reasons, that it is none of these things.

Among the various features Augustine assigns to the mind, one especially deserves further elaboration. It comes close to what has been familiarly called "privileged access." Gilbert Ryle characterizes it this way:

> Bodily processes and states can be inspected by external observers. So a man's bodily life is as much a public affair as are the lives of animals and reptiles and even as the careers of trees, crystals and planets. But . . . [the] workings of one mind are not witnessable by other observers; its career is private. Only I can take direct cognisance of the states and processes of my own mind.[2]

Compare Ryle's description of the idea of privileged access with this remarkable passage from Augustine's treatise on the origin of the soul, with which I began Chapter 4: "Although we are said to think in our heart, and although we know what our thoughts are, without the knowledge of any other person, yet we know not in what part of the body we have the heart itself, where we do our thinking, unless we are taught it by

2. *The Concept of Mind*, 11.

some other person, who yet is ignorant of what we think" (*On the Soul and Its Origin*, IV.6.7). Relying on scriptural locutions in which our thoughts are said to be in our heart, Augustine takes the heart to be the organ of thought. But the philosophical point is, if anything, underlined by this mistake. As for me, I take the brain to be the organ of thought. But I do not know where in my brain I think my thoughts, unless I am taught it by someone who is doubtless ignorant of what I am thinking.

These days philosophers tend to be rather judicious in making their claims of privileged access. Here is a very measured claim by Donald Davidson: ". . . sincere first person present-tense claims about thoughts, while neither infallible nor incorrigible, have an authority no second or third person claim, or first person other-tense claim, can have."[3] On the whole, Augustine's assertions of first-person authority concerning mental acts and states seem more in line with Davidsonian judiciousness than with the rather extreme assertion of privileged access Ryle criticizes. Here is a relevant passage: "It is you, O Lord, who judge me. For though no one can know a man's thoughts, except the man's own spirit that is within him [1 Corinthians 2:11], there are some things which even his own spirit within him does not know" (*Confessions*, X.5). A similar judiciousness commonly characterizes Augustine's other claims to know his own mind, as, for example, in this passage about knowing what he wills:

> . . . who would not regard: 'Perhaps you are deceived,' as an impudent reply to one who says: 'I will to be happy'? And if he were to say: 'I know that I will this, and I know that I know this,' then to these two he can also add a third, that he knows these two, and also a fourth, that he knows that he knows these two, and can likewise continue indefinitely. If someone were also to say: 'I do not will to err,' will it not be true that whether he errs or does not err, yet he does not will to err? Would it not be the

3. "Knowing One's Own Mind," Presidential Address, American Philosophical Association, *Proceedings and Addresses* 60 (1987), 441.

height of impudence for anyone to say to this man: 'Perhaps you are deceived,' since no matter in what he may be deceived, he is certainly not deceived in not willing to be deceived? (*Trinity*, XV.12.21)

Judicious or not, these are further examples of things that, according to Augustine, the mind can "perceive through itself." And they are brought out by asking, 'Can I be mistaken in thinking that I* will to be happy?' 'Can I be mistaken in thinking that I* do not will to err?'

ఆ

So what are we to say, in conclusion, about the role of thought's ego in the philosophies of Augustine and Descartes?

Simply put, it is thought's ego that directs Descartes's great rational reconstruction of knowledge. In a certain way Descartes also identifies himself with his thought's ego: he identifies himself with that being whose existence and nature are vouchsafed to him even on the supposition that all life is his dream and no bodies even exist.

For Augustine, thought's ego offers, first of all, a perspective from which to refute universal skepticism. In the absence of a solipsistic hypothesis, Augustine then supplements the work of thought's ego (i.e., 'I*' questions he raises) with "the mind's ego" (i.e., 'mind–it*' questions) to develop a concept of mind that prefigures Descartes's concept of mind.

As for a rational reconstruction of knowledge, Augustine has no such project, and therefore none directed from the viewpoint of thought's ego. The mature Augustine, in his role as philosopher, seems quite content to undertake something far more modest, namely, to seek a reflective appreciation of how it can be the case that p, for philosophically problematic claims that p. To many of us today, that relatively modest undertaking is quite challenging enough and, in any case, altogether worthy of a talented philosopher's most enviable talents.

The Rational Reconstruction
of Knowledge

What I call in this work "the rational reconstruction of knowledge" is something Descartes announces in the second sentence of his *Meditations,* in these words: "I realized that it was necessary, once in the course of my life, to demolish everything completely and start again right from the foundations if I wanted to establish anything at all in the sciences that was stable and likely to last" (AT VII, 17; CSM II, 12). This reconstruction is, I take it, the primary project of the *Meditations.* It is also presented in Part IV of the *Discourse* and in parts of the *Principles.*

This reconstruction project has both a methodological component and a substantive component. Prominent in the methodological component are these elements:

(i)   the method of systematic doubt (or method of hyperbolical doubt);
(ii)   the rule of clarity and distinctness; and
(iii) the coherence test (for telling whether one is now dreaming).

Prominent in the substantive component are these claims:

(1) I exist.
(2) I am a thinking thing (a mind).

(3)   God exists.
(4)   There is a real distinction between mind and body (mind–body dualism).
(5)   Material things exist.

Keeping to the building metaphor, we could say that Descartes treats the method of systematic doubt as a "clearing operation" ("I will devote myself sincerely and without reservation to the general demolition of my opinions") and also as a test for a foundation stone that will be firm. In terms of that same metaphor,

(1)   I exist

is Descartes's foundation stone (he describes it in the *Discourse* as "the first principle of the philosophy I was seeking").

Continuing with the building metaphor, we could say that, although Descartes has already rested

(2)   I am a thinking thing

very tentatively atop his foundation stone in Meditation II, it is not until he has established

(4)   There is a real distinction between mind and body

in Meditation VI that he "mortars" it permanently into place.

Descartes introduces the rule of clarity and distinctness in Meditation III as a product of reflecting on what makes his foundation stone so trustworthy: "In this first item of knowledge there is simply a clear and distinct perception of what I am asserting; this would not be enough to make me certain of the truth of the matter if it could ever turn out that something which I perceived with such clarity and distinctness was false" (AT VII, 35; CSM II, 24). But he attempts to validate it in Meditations IV and V. "Now, however, I have perceived that

God exists, and at the same time I have understood that everything else depends on him, and that he is no deceiver; and I have drawn the conclusion that everything which I clearly and distinctly perceive is of necessity true" (AT VII, 70; CSM II, 48).

Since Descartes, it seems, is not entitled to appeal to the existence and nature of God to underwrite the rule of clarity and distinctness until he has proved that God exists and is no deceiver, and since he apparently uses the rule of clarity and distinctness in proving God's existence and nature, commentators have charged him with circular reasoning in this matter. Much scholarly effort has been expended to determine whether there is a way to avoid this "Cartesian circle" and, if so, whether Descartes makes use of it.

The coherence test (for determining whether one is now dreaming) does not appear until the end of the *Meditations*. It does not appear at all in the *Discourse* or the *Principles*. It plays no role in validating any other knowledge claims in the *Meditations*. One might surmise that it is meant to be useful in the further reconstruction of knowledge each of us can carry out for ourselves, as when we go on to do physical science. Alternatively, one might conclude, as I suggest in Chapter 7, that it plays no significant role in the rational reconstruction of knowledge.

Bibliography

BOOKS

Alston, William P. *Epistemic Justification: Essays in the Theory of Knowledge*. Ithaca, N.Y.: Cornell University Press, 1989.

Anselm, *Basic Writings*, trans. S. N. Deane, LaSalle, Ill.: Open Court, 1961.

Blanchet, Léon, *Les antécédents historique du "Je pense, donc je suis."* Paris: Félix Alcan, 1920.

Bubacz, Bruce. *St. Augustine's Theory of Knowledge: A Contemporary Analysis*. New York: Edwin Mellen, 1981.

Chisholm, Roderick M. *Theory of Knowledge*. Englewood Cliffs, N.J.: Prentice-Hall, 1966.

——. *The First Person: An Essay on Reference and Intentionality*. Minneapolis: University of Minnesota Press, 1981.

Cicero. *De natura deorum*, trans. H. Rackham. Loeb Classical Library, Cambridge: Harvard University Press, 1933.

Curley, E. M. *Descartes against the Skeptics*. Cambridge: Harvard University Press, 1978.

Dulaey, Martine. *Le rêve dans la vie et la pensée de Saint Augustin*. Paris: Etudes Augustiniennes, 1973.

Feldman, Fred. *A Cartesian Introduction to Philosophy*. New York: McGraw-Hill, 1986.

Finocchiaro, Maurice A., ed. *The Galileo Affair: A Documentary History*. Berkeley: University of California Press, 1989.

Flasch, Kurt. *Augustin: Einführung in sein Denken.* Stuttgart: Reclam, 1980.

Frankfurt, Harry *Demons, Dreamers, and Madmen.* Indianapolis: Bobbs-Merrill, 1970.

Freud, Sigmund. *Collected Papers,* 5 vols. New York: Basic Books, 1959.

Geach, P. T. *Logic Matters.* Oxford: Blackwell, 1972.

Gilson, Etienne. *Index scolastico-cartésien.* Paris, 1912; reprinted: New York: Burt Franklin, Bibliography and Reference Series no. 57.

———. *Etude sur le rôle de la pensée mediévale dans la formation du système cartésien.* Paris: Vrin, 1930; 3d ed., 1967.

———. *The Christian Philosophy of Saint Augustine,* trans. L. E. M. Lynch. New York: Random House, 1960.

Gouhier, Henri. *Cartésianisme et Augustinisme au XVIIe siècle.* Paris: Vrin, 1978.

Hölscher, Ludger. *The Reality of the Mind: St. Augustine's Philosophical Arguments for the Human Soul as a Spiritual Substance.* London: Routledge & Kegan Paul, 1986.

Katz, Jerrold J. *Cogitations.* New York: Oxford University Press, 1986.

Kenny, Anthony. *Descartes: A Study of His Philosophy.* New York: Random House, 1968.

Kirwan, Christopher. *Augustine.* London: Routledge, 1989.

Lütke, Karl Heinrich, *"Auctoritas" bei Augustin.* Stuttgart: Kohlhammer Verlag, 1968.

Moore, G. E. *Philosophical Papers.* London: Allen and Unwin, 1959.

Nagel, Thomas. *The View from Nowhere.* New York: Oxford University Press, 1986.

Nash, Ronald H. *The Light of the Mind: St. Augustine's Theory of Knowledge.* Lexington: University Press of Kentucky, 1969.

O'Connell, Robert J. *St. Augustine's Confessions.* Cambridge: Harvard University Press, 1969.

O'Daly, Gerard. *Augustine's Philosophy of Mind.* Berkeley: University of California Press, 1987.

Plato. *Republic,* trans. G. M. A. Grube. Indianapolis: Hackett, 1974.

———. *Theaetetus,* trans. John McDowell. Oxford: Clarendon Press, 1973.

Russell, Bertrand. *Problems of Philosophy.* New York: Oxford University Press, 1959.

_____. *An Outline of Philosophy.* Cleveland: World Publishing Company, 1960.

Ryle, Gilbert. *The Concept of Mind.* London: Hutchinson's University Library, 1949.

Sorabji, Richard. *Time, Creation, and the Continuum.* London: Duckworth, 1983.

Spinoza, Baruch. *Ethics and Selected Letters,* trans. Samuel Shirley. Indianapolis: Hackett, 1982.

Stroud, Barry. *The Significance of Philosophical Scepticism.* New York: Oxford University Press, 1984.

Taylor, Charles. *Sources of the Self.* Cambridge: Harvard University Press, 1989.

Walsh, W. H. *Metaphysics.* London: Hutchinson University Library, 1963.

Williams, Bernard. *Descartes: The Project of Pure Enquiry.* Harmondsworth: Penguin, 1978.

Wilson, Margaret Dauler. *Descartes.* London: Routledge & Kegan Paul, 1978.

ARTICLES

Anscombe, G. E. M., "The First Person." In *Mind and Language,* ed. Samuel Guttenplan, 45–65. Oxford: Clarendon Press.

Burge, Tyler. "Individualism and the Mental," *Midwest Studies in Philosophy* 4 (1979), 73–121.

Burnyeat, M. F. "Idealism and Greek Philosophy: What Descartes Saw and Berkeley Missed," *Philosophical Review* 91 (1982), 3–40.

_____. "The Sceptic in His Place and Time." In *Philosophy in History,* ed. R. Rorty, J. B. Schneewind, and A. Skinner, 225–54. Cambridge: Cambridge University Press, 1984.

_____. "Wittgenstein and Augustine *De Magistro,*" *Proceedings of the Aristotelian Society.* suppl. vol., 1987, 1–24.

Castañeda, Hector-Neri. "He: A Study in the Logic of Self-Consciousness," *Ratio* 8 (1966), 130–57.

_____. "Indicators and Quasi-indicators," *American Philosophical Quarterly* 4 (1967), 85–100.

_____. "On the Logic of Attributions of Self-Knowledge to Others," *Journal of Philosophy* 65 (1968), 439–56.

Coughlan, M. J. "'Si Fallor, Sum' Revisited," *Augustinian Studies* 13 (1982), 145–50.

Davidson, Donald. "Knowing One's Own Mind," Presidential Address, American Philosophical Association. *Proceedings and Addresses* 60 (1987), 441–58.

Henze, Donald F. "Descartes on Other Minds," *Studies in the Philosophy of Mind*. American Philosophical Quarterly Monograph Series, no. 6 (1972), 41–56.

Hintikka, Jaakko. "*Cogito, ergo Sum:* Inference or Performance?" *Philosophical Review* 71 (1962), 3–32.

Jackson, B. Darrell. "The Theory of Signs in St. Augustine's *De Doctrina Christiana*." In *Augustine: A Collection of Critical Essays,* ed. R. A. Markus, 92–147. Garden City, N.Y.: Anchor, 1972.

Katz, Jerrold J. "Descartes's Cogito," *Pacific Philosophical Quarterly* 68 (1987), 175–96.

Kretzmann, Norman. "Faith Seeks, Understanding Finds." In *Christian Philosophy,* ed. Thomas P. Flint, 1–36. Notre Dame: University of Notre Dame Press, 1989.

Lewis, David. "Attitudes De Dicto and De Se," *Philosophical Review* 88 (1979), 513–43.

McNulty, T. Michael. "Augustine's Argument for the Existence of Other Souls," *Modern Schoolman* 48 (1970), 19–25.

Mann, William E. "Dreams of Immorality," *Philosophy* 58 (1983), 378–85.

Markus, R. A. "St. Augustine on Signs." In *Augustine: A Collection of Critical Essays,* ed. R. A. Markus, 61–91. Garden City, N.Y.: Anchor, 1972.

Matthews, Gareth B. "Augustine on Speaking from Memory," *American Philosophical Quarterly* 2 (1965), 157–60; reprinted in *Augustine: A Collection of Critical Essays,* ed. R. A. Markus, 168–75. Garden City, N.Y.: Doubleday, 1972.

———. "The Inner Man," *American Philosophical Quarterly* 4 (1967), 166–72; reprinted in *Augustine: A Collection of Critical Essays,* ed. R. A. Markus, Garden City, N.Y.: Doubleday, 1972.

———. "Bodily Motions and Religious Feelings," *Canadian Journal of Philosophy* 1 (1971), 75–86; reprinted in *Readings in the Philosophy of Religion: An Analytic Approach,* ed. B. A. Brody, 551–61. Englewood Cliffs, N.J.: Prentice-Hall, 1974.

_____. "*Si Fallor Sum.*" In *Augustine: A Collection of Critical Essays,* ed. R. A. Markus, 151–62. Garden City, N.Y.: Doubleday, 1972.

_____. "Consciousness and Life," *Philosophy* 52 (1977), 13–26; reprinted in *The Nature of Mind,* ed. David M. Rosenthal, 63–70. New York: Oxford University Press, 1991.

_____. "Animals and the Unity of Psychology," *Philosophy* 53 (1978), 437–54.

_____. "Ritual and the Religious Feelings." In *Explaining Emotions,* ed. A. O. Rorty, 337–53. Berkeley: University of California Press, 1980; reprinted in *Contemporary Philosophy of Religion,* ed. S. M. Cahn and D. Shatz, 154–66. New York: Oxford, 1981.

_____. "On Being Immoral in a Dream," *Philosophy* 56 (1981), 47–54.

_____. "Descartes and the Problem of Other Minds." In *Essays on Descartes' Meditations,* ed. A. Rorty, 141–51. Berkeley: University of California Press, 1986.

_____. "Descartes's *Cogito* and Katz's *Cogitations,*" *Pacific Philosophical Quarterly* 68 (1987), 197–204.

Perry, John. "The Essential Indexical," *Nous* 13 (1979), 3–21.

Triplett, Timm. "Recent Work on Foundationalism," *American Philosophical Quarterly* 27 (1990), 93–116.

Zellner, Harold. "Spinoza's Puzzle," *History of Philosophy Quarterly* 5 (1988), 233–43.

Index of Subjects

Index of Persons

Index of Passages

WORKS BY AUGUSTINE

WORKS BY DESCARTES

Library of Congress Cataloging-in-Publication Data

Matthews, Gareth B., 1929–
  Thought's ego in Augustine and Descartes / Gareth B. Matthews.
     p.   cm.
  Includes bibliographical references and index.
  ISBN 0-8014-2775-4 (alk. paper)
  1. Augustine, Saint, Bishop of Hippo.   2. Descartes, René, 1596–
1650.   I. Title.
B655.Z7M347   1992
189′.2—dc20   92-52767